I0004286

CLOUD MADE SIMPLE

YOUR FIRST STEPS IN MICROSOFT AZURE

FIRST EDITION

Preface

Cloud computing has transformed the way individuals and organizations think about, access, and manage computing resources. From flexible infrastructure provisioning to rapid software deployment, the cloud has enabled innovation at a pace never before possible. Yet, for newcomers and even seasoned IT professionals, the cloud can seem vast, complex, and at times overwhelming.

This book, *Mastering Microsoft Azure for Beginners*, serves as a foundational guide for anyone embarking on a journey into the world of cloud computing, particularly through the lens of Microsoft Azure — one of the leading cloud platforms in the industry. Whether you're an aspiring developer, a system administrator, a business analyst, or someone with a curiosity for emerging technologies, this book aims to provide a solid grounding in Azure's capabilities and how to leverage them effectively.

The journey begins with **Chapter 1**, where we demystify the cloud landscape. You'll learn what cloud computing really means, the benefits and trade-offs of moving to the cloud, and how to differentiate between service models like IaaS, PaaS, and SaaS. We'll also explore deployment models, and introduce major cloud providers, setting a broad context before narrowing in on Azure.

In **Chapter 2**, we dive directly into Microsoft Azure. You'll create your first account, explore the Azure Portal, and understand key organizational constructs like subscriptions and resource groups. This is where theory meets practice, and your Azure journey truly begins.

Chapter 3 offers a deep dive into core Azure services, explaining the essential components every cloud project will likely interact with — from virtual machines to databases, storage to identity services. These are the building blocks you'll use to construct cloud solutions.

Once you're familiar with the core, **Chapter 4** takes you hands-on with a project-oriented approach. You'll plan and build a small web application hosted in Azure, connect it to a database, and implement best practices for monitoring and resource management.

Security is critical in the cloud, and **Chapter 5** focuses on protecting your Azure environment. From role-based access control (RBAC) to encryption and compliance tools, this chapter is your first step toward secure cloud design.

Azure isn't just about technology; it's also about managing costs wisely. **Chapter 6** addresses pricing structures, budgeting tools, and techniques to optimize your cloud spend without compromising performance.

Things don't always go smoothly — and when they don't, **Chapter 7** helps you troubleshoot common problems, use diagnostics tools, and know when and how to seek Microsoft support.

In **Chapter 8**, we look ahead. You'll be introduced to DevOps principles, automated deployment with ARM templates, and how Azure supports modern workloads like AI and machine learning. We also guide you toward certifications and learning paths to take your Azure skills to the next level.

Finally, **Chapter 9** includes appendices with a glossary, additional resources, project ideas, an API guide, and answers to common questions. It's a ready-reference for continued learning and development.

We hope this book becomes your trusted companion as you navigate Azure and unlock the true potential of cloud computing. Let's get started.

Table of Contents

Chapter 1: Understanding the Cloud Landscape

What is Cloud Computing?

Cloud computing is a model for delivering information technology services where resources are retrieved from the internet through web-based tools and applications. Instead of owning their own computing infrastructure or data centers, companies can rent access to storage, applications, and processing power from a cloud service provider on an as-needed basis.

This model transforms traditional IT by enabling faster innovation, flexible resources, and economies of scale. The cloud removes the burden of owning and maintaining hardware, allowing organizations to focus more on their core objectives.

At its core, cloud computing is about accessing computing services — servers, storage, databases, networking, software, analytics, and intelligence — over the Internet ("the cloud") to offer faster innovation, flexible resources, and cost savings.

Let's unpack this further.

Key Characteristics of Cloud Computing

1. **On-Demand Self-Service**
   Users can provision computing resources like server time and network storage as needed automatically without requiring human interaction with the service provider.

2. **Broad Network Access**
   Resources are accessible over the network and available through standard mechanisms that promote use by heterogeneous thin or thick client platforms (e.g., mobile phones, tablets, laptops).

3. **Resource Pooling**
   The provider's computing resources are pooled to serve multiple consumers using a multi-tenant model, with different physical and virtual resources dynamically assigned and reassigned according to demand.

4. **Rapid Elasticity**
   Capabilities can be elastically provisioned and released, sometimes automatically, to scale rapidly outward and inward commensurate with demand.

5. **Measured Service**
   Cloud systems automatically control and optimize resource use by leveraging a metering capability appropriate to the type of service (e.g., storage, processing, bandwidth).

History and Evolution

The concept of cloud computing dates back to the 1960s when John McCarthy, a prominent computer scientist, suggested that "computation may someday be organized as a public utility." Fast forward to the 1990s and 2000s, advancements in internet bandwidth and virtualization technologies brought this idea to life.

Amazon launched its Elastic Compute Cloud (EC2) in 2006, widely considered the start of modern cloud computing. Microsoft Azure followed in 2010, alongside other providers like Google Cloud Platform. Today, the cloud is the backbone of digital transformation across all industries.

Cloud Computing Architecture

A typical cloud computing architecture consists of:

- **Front-end platforms**: the client device and interface (like a browser or app) used to access the cloud.

- **Back-end platforms**: servers, storage, and databases located in data centers.

- **Cloud-based delivery**: ensures high availability, scalability, and performance.

- **Network**: the internet or private networks connecting users to cloud services.

Types of Cloud Services

Cloud computing services can be broadly categorized into three service models:

- **Infrastructure as a Service (IaaS)**: Basic computing resources like virtual machines, networking, and storage.

- **Platform as a Service (PaaS)**: Tools and services that allow developers to build, deploy, and manage applications.

- **Software as a Service (SaaS)**: Ready-to-use software delivered over the internet.

Each model abstracts a different layer of the computing stack, allowing users to focus on what matters most to them while delegating other responsibilities to the cloud provider.

Real-World Examples

- **IaaS Example**: A startup uses Azure Virtual Machines to host their application, scaling up as user demand increases.

- **PaaS Example**: A developer uses Azure App Services and Azure SQL Database to build and deploy a web application quickly.

- **SaaS Example**: A company uses Microsoft 365 for collaboration, without managing any infrastructure.

Cloud Deployment Models

Understanding how cloud services are deployed is just as important as knowing what they are. There are three main deployment models:

- **Public Cloud**: Services are delivered over the public internet and shared among multiple users.

- **Private Cloud**: Infrastructure is dedicated to a single organization, often for security and compliance.

- **Hybrid Cloud**: Combines public and private clouds, allowing data and applications to move between them.

Advantages of Cloud Computing

1. **Cost Efficiency**: Pay only for what you use, eliminating capital expenses on hardware.

2. **Speed and Agility**: Provision new resources in minutes instead of weeks.

3. **Global Scale**: Serve users from data centers across the globe.

4. **Performance**: Benefit from regularly upgraded infrastructure.

5. **Security**: Leverage high-end security features and compliance certifications.

6. **Productivity**: Free up IT teams from maintenance tasks.

Challenges of Cloud Computing

1. **Downtime Risks**: Relying on third-party providers can be risky during outages.

2. **Security Concerns**: Data privacy and compliance require careful planning.

3. **Vendor Lock-in**: Transitioning between cloud providers can be complex.

4. **Hidden Costs**: Mismanagement can lead to unexpected bills.

5. **Complexity in Governance**: Managing multiple services, users, and policies requires robust governance frameworks.

The Future of Cloud Computing

Cloud computing continues to evolve rapidly. Emerging trends include:

- **Edge Computing**: Bringing computation closer to where data is generated.

- **Serverless Architectures**: Abstracting infrastructure management even further.

- **AI and Machine Learning**: Integrated into cloud platforms for intelligent applications.

- **Sustainability**: Eco-friendly data center initiatives and carbon-neutral commitments.

Getting Started with the Cloud

For beginners, the cloud may seem like a massive leap from traditional systems, but starting small is key. Begin by creating a free Azure account, experimenting with virtual machines, and deploying a simple web app. As confidence builds, so will your understanding and usage of the broader ecosystem.

Here's a simple example of deploying a virtual machine using Azure CLI:

```
az login
az group create --name MyResourceGroup --location eastus
az vm create \
  --resource-group MyResourceGroup \
  --name MyFirstVM \
  --image UbuntuLTS \
  --admin-username azureuser \
  --generate-ssh-keys
```

This script logs into your Azure account, creates a resource group, and spins up a virtual machine using a default Linux image.

Conclusion

Cloud computing is no longer a luxury — it's a necessity. Understanding what it is and how it works is crucial for anyone entering or currently working in the tech industry. This chapter has laid the groundwork for the rest of the book, which will focus specifically on Microsoft Azure and how to use it to build powerful, scalable, and efficient solutions.

Whether you're looking to modernize your skills or shift your organization's infrastructure to the cloud, this journey will equip you with the knowledge and confidence to make it happen.

Benefits and Challenges of Cloud Adoption

The shift to cloud computing is one of the most significant technological trends of the 21st century. Organizations of all sizes — from startups to multinational corporations — are embracing cloud services to accelerate innovation, reduce costs, and enhance scalability. However, adopting cloud technology also introduces a set of challenges that must be addressed to ensure a successful transformation.

This section provides an in-depth look at both the benefits and the challenges of moving to the cloud, giving you a comprehensive understanding of what to expect and how to prepare.

Strategic Benefits of Cloud Adoption

1. Cost Savings and Operational Efficiency

One of the most commonly cited advantages of cloud computing is the reduction in capital expenditure (CapEx). Traditional IT requires significant investment in physical hardware, data centers, and maintenance. With cloud services, you pay only for what you use, shifting to an operational expenditure (OpEx) model.

- **Elastic Pricing Models**: Cloud services like Azure offer pay-as-you-go pricing, subscription tiers, and reserved instances to fit various usage patterns.

- **Reduced Maintenance**: The responsibility of maintaining hardware and managing system updates falls to the cloud provider.

Example Scenario: An organization that previously maintained a data center for seasonal workloads can move these workloads to the cloud and scale them up or down as needed, avoiding the costs associated with underutilized infrastructure.

2. Scalability and Flexibility

Cloud platforms like Microsoft Azure enable automatic scaling, allowing you to increase or decrease resources based on demand.

- **Horizontal Scaling**: Adding more virtual machines or containers to distribute the load.

- **Vertical Scaling**: Increasing the resources (CPU, RAM) of an existing virtual machine.

This elasticity ensures optimal performance without over-provisioning.

```
az vm scale-set create \
  --resource-group MyGroup \
  --name MyScaleSet \
  --image UbuntuLTS \
  --upgrade-policy-mode automatic \
  --admin-username azureuser \
  --generate-ssh-keys
```

The command above creates a virtual machine scale set in Azure, automatically scaling based on the workload.

3. Speed and Agility

With cloud platforms, provisioning infrastructure is a matter of minutes, not weeks. This accelerates time-to-market for new features and services.

- **Rapid Development**: Use PaaS solutions to develop and deploy applications without worrying about the underlying hardware.

- **Experimentation**: Spin up resources quickly to test new ideas, then shut them down with minimal cost.

4. Innovation Enablement

Cloud platforms provide access to cutting-edge tools and services such as AI, machine learning, IoT, and advanced analytics. These services allow businesses to create smart applications and gain deep insights from their data.

- **Azure Cognitive Services**: Enables apps to see, hear, speak, and understand with AI.

- **Azure Synapse Analytics**: Unifies enterprise data integration, warehousing, and big data analytics.

5. Business Continuity and Disaster Recovery

The cloud offers robust backup and recovery solutions, ensuring minimal disruption in case of a disaster.

- **Geo-Redundancy**: Azure stores your data in multiple regions.

- **Automated Backups**: Simplify disaster recovery planning with tools like Azure Backup and Azure Site Recovery.

6. Security and Compliance

Despite common misconceptions, cloud platforms often provide a higher level of security than on-premises systems, especially for small to medium-sized organizations.

- **Advanced Security Controls**: Encryption at rest and in transit, identity and access management, network security groups.

- **Regulatory Compliance**: Azure complies with a broad set of international and industry-specific standards like ISO 27001, HIPAA, and GDPR.

Common Challenges in Cloud Adoption

While the benefits are significant, cloud adoption is not without hurdles. Understanding these challenges helps you plan strategically and avoid costly mistakes.

1. Cost Management and Overspending

Though cloud services can be more cost-effective than traditional IT, mismanagement can lead to runaway expenses.

- **Over-Provisioning**: Spinning up more resources than necessary.

- **Idle Resources**: Forgetting to decommission unused services.

- **Data Transfer Costs**: Moving data in and out of the cloud can incur significant fees.

Solution: Use Azure Cost Management + Billing to monitor and control spending. Set budgets, track usage, and analyze cost trends.

```
az consumption budget create \
  --amount 200 \
  --category cost \
  --name Budget2025 \
  --resource-group MyResourceGroup \
  --time-grain monthly \
  --time-period 'start=2025-01-01T00:00:00Z;end=2025-12-
31T23:59:59Z'
```

2. Security and Privacy Concerns

Migrating data to the cloud raises legitimate concerns about security, privacy, and regulatory compliance.

- **Data Breaches**: Misconfigured services or access policies can expose sensitive data.

- **Shared Responsibility Model**: While the cloud provider secures the infrastructure, you are responsible for securing your data, access controls, and applications.

Solution: Implement identity management tools like Azure Active Directory, use role-based access control (RBAC), and apply encryption throughout.

3. Vendor Lock-in

Once an organization becomes heavily reliant on a particular cloud provider's services and APIs, switching providers or going multi-cloud can be complex and expensive.

Solution: Design your architecture with portability in mind. Favor open standards, containerized applications (e.g., Docker, Kubernetes), and abstracted APIs when possible.

4. Migration Complexity

Moving legacy systems and workloads to the cloud is rarely a lift-and-shift operation. It often requires rearchitecting applications, changing workflows, and training staff.

- **Dependency Mapping**: Understanding how systems interact is crucial before migration.

- **Downtime Risks**: Poorly planned migrations can result in outages.

Solution: Use tools like Azure Migrate to assess readiness and automate migration planning.

5. Skill Gaps and Cultural Resistance

Adopting cloud services often demands new skills, roles, and ways of working. Organizations may face internal resistance or lack the necessary expertise.

- **Cloud-Native Skills**: DevOps, infrastructure as code, automation, and containerization are essential.

- **Mindset Shift**: From owning infrastructure to renting and scaling dynamically.

Solution: Invest in training, certifications (e.g., Microsoft Certified: Azure Fundamentals), and promote a culture of continuous learning.

6. Governance and Compliance

As cloud environments scale, enforcing governance policies becomes more complex. Without proper oversight, you risk non-compliance and security vulnerabilities.

- **Shadow IT**: Departments deploying their own resources without centralized oversight.

- **Policy Drift**: Environments evolve in ways that diverge from security baselines.

Solution: Use Azure Policy to enforce rules and Azure Blueprints to standardize deployments.

```
az policy definition create \
  --name restrict-location \
  --rules 'location-policy.json' \
  --display-name "Restrict Locations" \
  --mode All
```

Best Practices for Successful Cloud Adoption

To fully realize the benefits and minimize the risks, organizations should consider the following best practices:

1. **Establish a Cloud Center of Excellence (CCoE)**
   A CCoE is a dedicated team responsible for guiding cloud adoption, setting standards, and ensuring best practices are followed.

2. **Define a Cloud Adoption Strategy**
   Align cloud initiatives with business goals. Identify which workloads make sense to move and in what order.

3. **Start with Low-Risk Projects**
   Begin cloud adoption with non-critical applications to gain experience and refine your strategy.

4. **Use Infrastructure as Code (IaC)**
   Manage and provision resources using templates and automation tools like Azure Resource Manager (ARM), Bicep, or Terraform.

5. **Regularly Audit and Optimize**
   Continuously monitor performance, security, and costs to identify areas for improvement.

6. **Empower Teams**
   Provide teams with self-service capabilities while maintaining guardrails to ensure compliance and cost control.

7. **Plan for Hybrid and Multi-Cloud**
   Even if you start with a single provider, be aware of strategies to integrate on-

premises or additional cloud platforms in the future.

Real-World Case Study: Cloud Success and Pitfalls

A medium-sized retail company decided to move their ecommerce platform to Azure to handle growing traffic during holiday seasons. They successfully reduced infrastructure costs by 40% using autoscaling virtual machines and Azure CDN.

However, they initially neglected to set budget alerts and over-provisioned resources, leading to an unexpected bill. After implementing Azure Cost Management and training their teams on cloud best practices, they regained control and optimized their environment.

This example highlights both the immediate benefits and the learning curve associated with cloud adoption.

Conclusion

Cloud adoption can deliver transformative value to businesses of all sizes — but only when approached with clear strategy, understanding, and governance. From cost savings and rapid innovation to global scale and enhanced security, the advantages are substantial. However, missteps in migration planning, cost management, or security posture can negate these benefits.

By acknowledging and planning for the challenges early, organizations can successfully navigate their cloud journey. As we move deeper into this book, you'll learn how Microsoft Azure addresses these challenges and provides tools to ensure a smooth, secure, and scalable cloud experience.

Key Cloud Service Models (IaaS, PaaS, SaaS)

Cloud computing is built on several foundational service models that abstract and deliver different layers of computing functionality over the internet. These service models allow organizations to select the appropriate level of control, flexibility, and management for their applications and infrastructure. The three primary service models are:

- Infrastructure as a Service (IaaS)

- Platform as a Service (PaaS)

- Software as a Service (SaaS)

Each model caters to specific use cases and offers varying levels of abstraction and responsibility. Understanding these models is crucial to selecting the right architecture, estimating costs, and defining team responsibilities.

Infrastructure as a Service (IaaS)

IaaS provides virtualized computing resources over the internet. It serves as the foundational building block of cloud computing, offering users access to networking, storage, and virtual machines (VMs), while the cloud provider manages the physical hardware and virtualization layer.

Characteristics of IaaS:

- Full control over virtual machines, networking, and operating systems.

- Users are responsible for configuring and managing operating systems, runtime environments, and applications.

- Highly flexible and scalable — ideal for dynamic workloads.

Common Use Cases:

- Hosting websites and web apps.

- Developing and testing environments.

- High-performance computing and big data processing.

- Custom enterprise applications with complex infrastructure needs.

Azure Examples:

- **Azure Virtual Machines**: On-demand scalable computing.

- **Azure Virtual Network**: Isolated networks with subnets, IPs, and gateways.

- **Azure Load Balancer**: Distributes incoming traffic among VMs.

- **Azure Disk Storage**: Persistent and high-performance storage for VMs.

IaaS Example: Provisioning a VM with Azure CLI

```
az vm create \
  --name MyAppVM \
  --resource-group IaaSGroup \
  --image UbuntuLTS \
  --admin-username cloudadmin \
  --generate-ssh-keys
```

This command provisions an Ubuntu VM on Azure, giving full control to the user to install and manage software, configure firewalls, and deploy services.

Pros of IaaS:

- Maximum control and customization.
- Pay-as-you-go model reduces upfront costs.
- Quick provisioning of new environments.
- Suitable for lift-and-shift migrations.

Cons of IaaS:

- Requires technical expertise to configure and maintain.
- Users are responsible for patching and updating systems.
- Potential for misconfiguration and security risks.

Platform as a Service (PaaS)

PaaS provides a higher level of abstraction, allowing users to build, test, and deploy applications without managing the underlying infrastructure. It includes operating systems, development tools, database management, and runtime environments.

Characteristics of PaaS:

- Focuses on the development and deployment lifecycle.
- Abstracts away server management, OS updates, and patching.
- Offers built-in services for scalability, availability, and integration.

Common Use Cases:

- Web and mobile application development.
- Microservices and APIs.
- Continuous Integration / Continuous Deployment (CI/CD) workflows.

- Business analytics and data processing applications.

Azure Examples:

- **Azure App Service**: Deploy web apps using .NET, Node.js, Java, Python, and more.

- **Azure Functions**: Serverless compute that responds to events.

- **Azure SQL Database**: Fully managed relational database service.

- **Azure Logic Apps**: Automate workflows and integrate services.

PaaS Example: Deploying a Web App with Azure CLI

```
az webapp up \
  --name mywebapp12345 \
  --resource-group PaaSGroup \
  --runtime "NODE|16-lts" \
  --location eastus
```

This command automatically provisions an App Service plan and deploys your app using the Node.js runtime, removing the need to manage VMs or servers.

Pros of PaaS:

- Accelerates development cycles.

- Simplifies deployment and scaling.

- Integrated DevOps and CI/CD tooling.

- Built-in load balancing, monitoring, and security features.

Cons of PaaS:

- Less control over the environment and configuration.

- Platform limitations and restrictions.

- Potential for vendor lock-in.

Software as a Service (SaaS)

SaaS delivers fully functional applications over the internet, typically on a subscription basis. End users access the software via web browsers or mobile apps without worrying about installation, infrastructure, or updates.

Characteristics of SaaS:

- No need to install or maintain software locally.

- Accessible from any internet-connected device.

- Software updates and maintenance are managed by the provider.

Common Use Cases:

- Email and collaboration platforms.

- Customer relationship management (CRM).

- Enterprise resource planning (ERP).

- File storage and sharing services.

Azure and Microsoft SaaS Examples:

- **Microsoft 365**: Email, Office apps, and collaboration tools.

- **Dynamics 365**: CRM and ERP platform.

- **Power BI**: Business analytics as a service.

- **Azure DevOps Services**: Hosted development tools.

SaaS Example: Using Microsoft 365

An organization can subscribe to Microsoft 365 for access to Outlook, Word, Excel, and Teams, all hosted in the cloud. No setup is required beyond account creation, and updates are automatically applied.

Pros of SaaS:

- Minimal effort for deployment and maintenance.

- Predictable costs with monthly or yearly subscriptions.

- Access from anywhere, on any device.

- Easy scalability and collaboration.

Cons of SaaS:

- Limited customization.

- Data control and privacy depend on the provider.

- Integration with legacy systems may be challenging.

Comparing IaaS, PaaS, and SaaS

Feature	IaaS	PaaS	SaaS
User Control	OS, middleware, apps	Apps and data only	Just app usage
Provider Responsibility	Networking, storage, servers	Runtime, OS, infrastructure	Everything
Flexibility	High	Medium	Low
Setup Complexity	High	Medium	Low
Use Case Example	Hosting custom databases	Deploying APIs	Using Microsoft 365
Target Users	Sysadmins, IT departments	Developers	End-users

Choosing the Right Model

The decision to choose IaaS, PaaS, or SaaS depends on various factors, including:

- **Technical Expertise**: Does your team have the skills to manage infrastructure?

- **Speed to Market**: Do you need to deploy quickly with minimal setup?

- **Customization Needs**: How much control do you need over the environment?

- **Compliance Requirements**: Are there specific data handling and security standards you must meet?

Often, businesses adopt a hybrid approach, combining multiple models:

- Using **IaaS** for legacy systems.

- Deploying new apps via **PaaS** for faster development.

- Relying on **SaaS** for internal productivity tools.

Real-World Example: Multi-Model Strategy

A healthcare startup may use:

- **IaaS** to run a legacy billing engine with full network control.

- **PaaS** to develop and host a patient-facing mobile app that accesses medical data via APIs.

- **SaaS** tools like Microsoft 365 and Power BI for office collaboration and analytics.

This layered approach ensures flexibility, optimizes cost, and minimizes operational burden.

Evolving Service Models

In addition to the primary service models, new paradigms are emerging:

- **FaaS (Function as a Service)**: Also known as serverless, where developers deploy functions that run in response to events (e.g., Azure Functions).

- **BaaS (Backend as a Service)**: Managed backend services for mobile and web apps.

- **DaaS (Desktop as a Service)**: Cloud-hosted desktops accessible from any device.

As cloud computing matures, these offerings are reshaping how we think about building and deploying applications.

Conclusion

Understanding the different cloud service models is essential for designing effective cloud solutions. Each model offers a different balance of control, responsibility, and convenience.

- **IaaS** is best when full control and flexibility are needed.

- **PaaS** is ideal for development-focused teams looking to deploy quickly.

- **SaaS** delivers out-of-the-box functionality with minimal overhead.

By selecting the right model for the right use case, organizations can optimize performance, control costs, and accelerate their journey to the cloud. As we progress through the chapters, you'll see how these models are implemented in Microsoft Azure and how to choose the right tools for your specific scenarios.

Public vs. Private vs. Hybrid Clouds

When adopting cloud computing, choosing the right deployment model is just as important as selecting the right service model. The deployment model defines how cloud resources are delivered, managed, and accessed — and significantly influences performance, security, scalability, compliance, and cost.

There are three primary cloud deployment models, each suited for specific needs and scenarios:

- **Public Cloud**

- **Private Cloud**

- **Hybrid Cloud**

In this section, we explore each model in depth, examining their characteristics, advantages, drawbacks, and typical use cases. We'll also look at how Microsoft Azure supports these models and how organizations can leverage them effectively.

Public Cloud

The **Public Cloud** model refers to cloud services delivered over the public internet and shared across multiple customers (tenants). The cloud provider owns and manages the infrastructure, while customers rent or subscribe to the services they need.

Characteristics:

- Services are hosted in the provider's data centers and accessed via the internet.

- Resources are shared among multiple organizations, though securely isolated.

- Customers pay for the services they use, often in a pay-as-you-go format.

- Requires minimal or no capital investment.

Advantages:

1. **Cost Efficiency**
   No need to invest in physical infrastructure. Organizations pay only for what they use.

2. **Scalability**
   Virtually unlimited scalability based on demand. Easily handle traffic spikes or growing workloads.

3. **High Availability**
   Cloud providers offer built-in redundancy and global distribution to ensure uptime.

4. **Faster Time to Market**
   Quickly deploy services and applications without long procurement or setup cycles.

5. **Maintenance-Free**
   The cloud provider manages updates, patching, and hardware maintenance.

Common Use Cases:

- Hosting websites and blogs.

- Application development and testing.

- Disaster recovery and backup.

- SaaS delivery (e.g., email, collaboration tools).

Azure Public Cloud Example:

Provisioning a globally available web application:

```
az webapp up \
  --name mypublicwebapp \
  --resource-group PublicCloudRG \
  --runtime "DOTNETCORE|7.0" \
```

```
--location westus2
```

This command creates and deploys a web app on Azure's public cloud infrastructure using .NET Core.

Challenges:

- **Security Concerns**: Data resides in a shared environment, which may raise privacy and compliance issues.

- **Limited Control**: Less customization compared to private infrastructure.

- **Data Residency**: Jurisdictional regulations may require data to stay within specific geographic boundaries.

Private Cloud

The **Private Cloud** model involves cloud infrastructure used exclusively by a single organization. It can be physically located on-premises or hosted by a third party but is not shared with other tenants.

Characteristics:

- Provides enhanced control over infrastructure, security, and compliance.

- Can be hosted internally (on-premises) or externally via a dedicated environment.

- Offers cloud capabilities like virtualization and resource pooling, but for a single entity.

Advantages:

1. **Greater Control and Customization**
   Organizations can tailor the infrastructure to meet specific needs.

2. **Improved Security and Compliance**
   Sensitive data stays behind the corporate firewall, easing compliance with regulations like HIPAA or GDPR.

3. **Integration with Legacy Systems**
   Easier to integrate with on-premises databases, ERP systems, and internal tools.

4. **Performance Optimization**
   Dedicated hardware eliminates noisy neighbor issues and ensures consistent

performance.

Common Use Cases:

- Financial institutions needing to meet strict regulatory requirements.

- Government agencies requiring high levels of data protection.

- Enterprises with existing data centers looking to modernize.

Azure Private Cloud Example:

While Azure is primarily a public cloud, Azure Stack allows you to bring Azure services to your own data center, creating a true private cloud:

```
# Azure Stack Hub deployment is done via the Azure portal or OEM-
specific tools
# Example: Use Azure Stack Development Kit (ASDK) for testing
private cloud on-prem
```

Challenges:

- **High Initial Cost**: Requires significant capital expenditure and ongoing maintenance.

- **Resource Limitations**: Scalability is constrained by internal infrastructure capacity.

- **Complex Management**: Organizations are responsible for managing the full stack, from hardware to applications.

Hybrid Cloud

The **Hybrid Cloud** model blends public and private cloud environments, allowing data and applications to be shared between them. It provides the flexibility to run sensitive workloads in a private cloud while leveraging the scalability of the public cloud.

Characteristics:

- Combines on-premises infrastructure or private cloud with public cloud services.

- Facilitates seamless data and application portability.

- Ideal for gradual cloud migration or integrating legacy systems with modern cloud apps.

Advantages:

1. **Flexibility and Scalability**
   Scale out to the public cloud when additional capacity is needed, without overprovisioning on-prem resources.

2. **Business Continuity and Disaster Recovery**
   Use public cloud for backup and failover while keeping primary systems in-house.

3. **Cost Optimization**
   Keep critical data on private systems while moving variable workloads to cost-effective public cloud environments.

4. **Regulatory Compliance**
   Store sensitive data on-prem while taking advantage of public cloud compute for less sensitive operations.

Common Use Cases:

- Healthcare providers storing patient data locally while analyzing anonymized data in the cloud.

- Retail companies using public cloud for seasonal sales spikes.

- Enterprises transitioning from legacy data centers to full cloud operations.

Azure Hybrid Cloud Example:

Using Azure Arc to manage on-prem and cloud resources from a single pane of glass:

```
az connectedmachine connect \
  --resource-group HybridCloudRG \
  --name OnPremServer1 \
  --location eastus
```

This command connects an on-premises server to Azure using Azure Arc, enabling hybrid management, monitoring, and policy application.

Challenges:

- **Integration Complexity**: Ensuring seamless interoperability between environments can be technically challenging.

- **Security and Governance**: Must maintain consistent security and policy enforcement across both clouds.

- **Latency and Data Movement**: Transferring data between on-prem and cloud can introduce latency and cost.

Decision Matrix: Choosing the Right Model

Requirement	Public Cloud	Private Cloud	Hybrid Cloud
Fast deployment	✓	✗	✓
High scalability	✓	✗	✓
Data residency control	✗	✓	✓
Regulatory compliance	✗	✓	✓
Cost-effectiveness for small orgs	✓	✗	✓
Integration with legacy systems	✗	✓	✓
Full control over infrastructure	✗	✓	✓
Flexibility and risk mitigation	✗	✗	✓

Real-World Scenario: Retail Cloud Strategy

A global retail company adopted a hybrid cloud approach to optimize their operations. Here's how they did it:

- **Private Cloud**: Core ERP and customer data were hosted on-premises due to strict regulatory requirements in certain countries.

- **Public Cloud**: Seasonal campaigns and e-commerce workloads were deployed in Azure for rapid scalability.

- **Hybrid Tools**: Azure ExpressRoute provided dedicated connections to Azure, ensuring low-latency communication between environments. Azure Arc unified the management layer.

The result was a highly optimized, scalable infrastructure that reduced costs and met compliance needs without sacrificing agility.

Tools Supporting Hybrid Deployments in Azure

- **Azure Arc**: Extend Azure management to on-premises, multicloud, and edge environments.

- **Azure Stack Hub/Edge/HCI**: Bring Azure services to your data center or edge locations.

- **Azure ExpressRoute**: Dedicated, private connection to Azure with higher security and performance.

- **Azure Site Recovery**: Enable disaster recovery between private and public clouds.

Evolving Cloud Models: Toward Multi-Cloud and Edge

The cloud landscape continues to evolve with emerging strategies:

- **Multi-Cloud**: Using services from multiple cloud providers (e.g., Azure + AWS + GCP) to avoid vendor lock-in and optimize services.

- **Edge Computing**: Deploying compute power closer to where data is generated to reduce latency and bandwidth usage.

Microsoft supports these models through:

- **Azure Arc-enabled Kubernetes**: Manage Kubernetes clusters anywhere.

- **Azure IoT Edge**: Deploy containerized workloads on IoT devices.

Conclusion

Selecting the right cloud deployment model is foundational to successful cloud adoption.

- The **Public Cloud** is ideal for organizations looking for rapid deployment, scalability, and cost-efficiency.

- The **Private Cloud** caters to enterprises needing tight control, high security, and compliance.

- The **Hybrid Cloud** offers the best of both worlds — enabling flexibility, risk mitigation, and strategic workload placement.

With Azure, organizations are not locked into a single model. Microsoft provides a broad range of tools and services that support all three deployment paradigms, helping you build a cloud environment that matches your technical and business requirements.

Understanding the nuances of each model ensures that you make informed decisions, architect resilient systems, and derive maximum value from your cloud investments.

Introduction to Major Cloud Providers

In the rapidly evolving digital world, cloud computing is no longer a niche service — it's the backbone of modern IT infrastructure. Organizations around the globe rely on cloud services for computing power, data storage, networking, machine learning, analytics, and more. While there are dozens of cloud service providers, a few dominate the global market due to their scale, breadth of services, reliability, and ecosystem maturity.

This section provides an in-depth overview of the major players in the cloud space, examining their strengths, service offerings, pricing models, certifications, global presence, and key differentiators. The most prominent cloud providers are:

- Microsoft Azure

- Amazon Web Services (AWS)

- Google Cloud Platform (GCP)

- IBM Cloud

- Oracle Cloud Infrastructure (OCI)

- Alibaba Cloud

We'll primarily focus on Azure as the book's core subject but will provide ample context for understanding how it compares to and interacts with other providers.

Microsoft Azure

Overview
Microsoft Azure, launched in 2010, is one of the world's leading cloud platforms. It offers a comprehensive suite of over 200 products and cloud services, including infrastructure, platform, and software solutions. It serves enterprises, governments, and developers worldwide.

Strengths:

- Seamless integration with Microsoft products (e.g., Windows Server, Active Directory, SQL Server, Microsoft 365).

- Enterprise-grade hybrid cloud capabilities through Azure Stack and Azure Arc.

- Deep investments in AI, DevOps, and analytics.

- Extensive security certifications and global compliance.

Key Offerings:

- **Azure Virtual Machines** (IaaS)

- **Azure App Services** (PaaS)

- **Azure Functions** (Serverless)

- **Azure Active Directory** (Identity and Access)

- **Azure Kubernetes Service** (Containers)

- **Azure Synapse Analytics** (Big Data & Analytics)

CLI Example: Creating a resource group in Azure

```
az group create --name AzureGroup --location eastus
```

Global Presence:
Microsoft Azure has over 60+ regions, with each region containing multiple data centers. It offers data residency options to comply with international regulations.

Pricing Model:
Azure operates on a pay-as-you-go model, with options for reserved instances and spot pricing. Pricing calculators and cost management tools are available via the portal.

Amazon Web Services (AWS)

Overview
Launched in 2006, AWS is the pioneer of modern cloud computing and remains the largest provider in terms of market share and global footprint. AWS provides a massive catalog of services for computing, storage, machine learning, and IoT.

Strengths:

- Market leader with extensive experience and support.

- Broadest range of services (over 200 fully featured services).

- High scalability, reliability, and availability.

- Strong developer and open-source community backing.

Key Offerings:

- **EC2** (Elastic Compute Cloud)

- **S3** (Simple Storage Service)

- **RDS** (Relational Database Service)

- **Lambda** (Serverless Computing)

- **CloudFormation** (Infrastructure as Code)

- **CloudWatch** (Monitoring and Logging)

CLI Example: Launching an EC2 instance

```
aws ec2 run-instances \
  --image-id ami-0abcdef1234567890 \
  --count 1 \
  --instance-type t2.micro \
  --key-name MyKeyPair \
  --security-groups MySecurityGroup
```

Global Presence:
AWS is available in 30+ regions with over 99 availability zones globally.

Pricing Model:
Pay-as-you-go with extensive discounts for reserved and spot instances. AWS also offers a Free Tier for new customers.

Google Cloud Platform (GCP)

Overview
GCP is Google's entry into the cloud space, officially launched in 2008. GCP leverages Google's experience in handling global-scale infrastructure and specializes in analytics, machine learning, and Kubernetes.

Strengths:

- Industry-leading AI/ML services.

- High-performance network infrastructure.

- Native Kubernetes support with Google Kubernetes Engine (GKE).

- Seamless integration with Google Workspace (formerly G Suite).

Key Offerings:

- **Compute Engine** (VMs)

- **App Engine** (PaaS)

- **Cloud Functions** (Serverless)

- **BigQuery** (Analytics)

- **Cloud AI Platform** (Machine Learning)

CLI Example: Creating a VM instance on GCP

```
gcloud compute instances create gcp-vm \
  --zone=us-central1-a \
  --machine-type=e2-medium \
  --image-family=debian-11 \
  --image-project=debian-cloud
```

Global Presence:
GCP has 35+ regions and more than 100 edge locations. Its global fiber network ensures low-latency connectivity.

Pricing Model:
GCP's pricing is known for its transparency and includes per-second billing. Sustained-use and committed-use discounts help reduce costs over time.

IBM Cloud

Overview
IBM Cloud focuses on providing hybrid cloud and AI-driven solutions to enterprises. With its acquisition of Red Hat, IBM has strengthened its open-source and Kubernetes strategy.

Strengths:

- Enterprise-grade hybrid cloud and AI tools.

- Focus on regulated industries (finance, healthcare).

- Integration with Watson AI services.

- Strong support for containers and OpenShift.

Key Offerings:

- **IBM Cloud Virtual Servers**

- **IBM Cloud Foundry**

- **IBM Kubernetes Service**

- **Watson Studio** (AI/ML Development)

- **Cloud Pak for Data**

CLI Example: Logging in and listing services

```
ibmcloud login --apikey <your_api_key>
ibmcloud resource service-instances
```

Global Presence:
IBM Cloud operates in 20+ availability zones across North America, Europe, and Asia.

Pricing Model:
Subscription-based and pay-as-you-go options with enterprise support tiers.

Oracle Cloud Infrastructure (OCI)

Overview
OCI is Oracle's next-generation cloud platform, built to run enterprise workloads, especially Oracle applications and databases, with high performance and security.

Strengths:

- Best-in-class support for Oracle databases.

- Strong SLAs and security compliance.

- Competitive pricing with predictable costs.

- Dedicated cloud regions for specific industries.

Key Offerings:

- **Oracle Compute** (VMs and Bare Metal)

- **Oracle Autonomous Database**

- **Oracle Cloud at Customer** (On-prem cloud services)

- **Oracle Functions**

- **Oracle Kubernetes Engine**

CLI Example: Creating a virtual machine instance

```
oci compute instance launch \
  --availability-domain <domain> \
  --compartment-id <compartment_id> \
  --shape VM.Standard2.1 \
  --image-id <image_id>
```

Global Presence:
OCI spans over 40 cloud regions and offers dedicated cloud infrastructure for government and financial customers.

Pricing Model:
Simple and predictable pricing models with BYOL (Bring Your Own License) options for Oracle software.

Alibaba Cloud

Overview
Alibaba Cloud, also known as Aliyun, is the leading cloud provider in China and rapidly expanding in Asia-Pacific, the Middle East, and Europe.

Strengths:

- Strong presence in Asia and emerging markets.

- Extensive support for ecommerce, logistics, and fintech.

- Integrated with Alibaba's ecosystem.

Key Offerings:

- **Elastic Compute Service (ECS)**

- **Object Storage Service (OSS)**

- **Alibaba Cloud Container Service**

- **MaxCompute** (Big Data platform)

- **Machine Learning Platform for AI**

CLI Example: Starting an ECS instance

```
aliyun ecs CreateInstance \
  --RegionId cn-hangzhou \
  --InstanceType ecs.t5-lc2m1.nano \
  --ImageId ubuntu_20_04_x64_20G_alibase_20230113.vhd
```

Global Presence:
More than 27 regions and 80 availability zones globally, with deep penetration in Asia.

Pricing Model:
Flexible pay-as-you-go pricing with regional discounts and enterprise support plans.

Comparison of Major Cloud Providers

Feature/Provider	Azure	AWS	GCP	IBM Cloud	OCI	Alibaba Cloud
Market Share	2nd	1st	3rd	Niche	Niche	Leading in Asia
Strength	Hybrid & MSFT	Breadth & Scale	ML & Analytics	Hybrid AI	Enterprise DBs	APAC Strength
VM Services	Azure VM	EC2	Compute Engine	Virtual Servers	Compute	ECS
Container Support	AKS	EKS	GKE	OpenShift	Kubernetes	Container Service
AI/ML Offerings	Azure AI	SageMaker	Cloud AI	Watson AI	Limited	MLPAI
Hybrid Tools	Arc/Stack	Outposts	Anthos	Satellite	Cloud@Customer	Local Zones
Global Regions	60+	30+	35+	20+	40+	27+
CLI Available	Yes	Yes	Yes	Yes	Yes	Yes

Multi-Cloud and Interoperability Trends

Organizations are increasingly adopting **multi-cloud** strategies to mitigate risks, avoid vendor lock-in, and use best-of-breed services. Cloud providers are responding with improved interoperability and tools that integrate across platforms.

Microsoft Azure + GCP Example:
Using Terraform or Azure Arc to manage resources across Azure and GCP from a single interface.

AWS + Azure Example:
Deploying services across AWS and Azure using containerization, Kubernetes federation, and cross-cloud VPNs.

Conclusion

The cloud ecosystem is rich with innovation and variety. While Microsoft Azure is a leader — especially in hybrid solutions, enterprise integration, and global reach — each provider brings unique value to the table.

Understanding the strengths, offerings, and positioning of these major players equips you to make strategic decisions about architecture, partnerships, and investments. As you progress through the book, Azure will take center stage, but keep in mind that knowledge of other platforms enhances your versatility and prepares you for real-world multi-cloud environments.

Chapter 2: Getting Started with Microsoft Azure

Overview of Microsoft Azure

Microsoft Azure is a comprehensive cloud computing platform and infrastructure created by Microsoft for building, deploying, and managing applications and services through a global network of data centers. It provides a vast and continually growing collection of integrated cloud services, including computing, networking, databases, analytics, storage, identity, security, and more.

Azure serves as the foundation for digital transformation in businesses around the world, enabling innovation at speed and scale while offering flexible consumption models. Azure supports a broad range of operating systems, programming languages, frameworks, databases, and devices — making it one of the most inclusive platforms on the market.

The Origin and Evolution of Azure

Azure was first announced in 2008 and officially launched in 2010 as "Windows Azure." Initially focused on PaaS (Platform as a Service), Azure expanded rapidly to include IaaS, SaaS, and hybrid cloud solutions. Microsoft rebranded it to "Microsoft Azure" in 2014 to reflect its broad capabilities beyond Windows-based services.

Today, Azure is a cornerstone of Microsoft's cloud-first strategy, with continued investment in AI, machine learning, edge computing, and hybrid models. Microsoft also places a strong emphasis on security, compliance, and enterprise readiness, making Azure a preferred choice for regulated industries such as finance, healthcare, and government.

Azure's Core Capabilities

Azure offers hundreds of services categorized into several key domains. Here are the main areas:

1. Compute

Azure provides scalable compute resources to run applications, host websites, or power data processing tasks.

- **Virtual Machines (VMs)**: Full control over Windows/Linux OS.

- **App Services**: Simplified PaaS hosting for web apps and APIs.

- **Azure Functions**: Serverless compute for event-driven logic.

- **Azure Kubernetes Service (AKS)**: Container orchestration and management.

2. Storage

Persistent, scalable, and secure data storage is a core requirement for any cloud platform.

- **Blob Storage**: Unstructured data, ideal for images, videos, and documents.

- **Disk Storage**: Persistent storage for VMs.

- **File Storage**: Managed file shares via SMB protocol.

- **Archive Storage**: Low-cost storage for infrequently accessed data.

3. Networking

Azure provides a robust network infrastructure to connect and secure your workloads.

- **Virtual Network (VNet)**: Isolated networks with subnets and custom IP ranges.

- **Azure Load Balancer**: Distributes incoming traffic.

- **Application Gateway**: Application-level routing and web application firewall.

- **ExpressRoute**: Dedicated private connectivity from on-prem to Azure.

4. Databases

Azure offers fully managed database services across SQL, NoSQL, and in-memory technologies.

- **Azure SQL Database**

- **Cosmos DB**

- **Azure Database for MySQL/PostgreSQL**

- **Redis Cache**

5. Identity and Security

Identity, governance, and protection services help secure your environment.

- **Azure Active Directory (AAD)**

- **Microsoft Defender for Cloud**

- **Azure Key Vault**

- **Azure Policy and RBAC**

6. Analytics and AI

Azure helps you derive insights from your data and build intelligent solutions.

- **Azure Synapse Analytics**

- **Power BI**

- **Cognitive Services**

- **Azure Machine Learning**

Azure Service Categories

Azure organizes services into logical categories:

Category	Examples
Compute	Azure VMs, App Service, AKS
Storage	Blob, Disk, Files, Queues
Networking	VNet, Load Balancer, DNS, ExpressRoute
Databases	SQL Database, Cosmos DB, Redis
Web & Mobile	Web Apps, Notification Hubs, API Management
AI & Machine Learning	Azure ML, Bot Services, Cognitive Services
DevOps	Azure DevOps, GitHub, Pipelines

Security	Defender for Cloud, Sentinel, Key Vault
IoT	IoT Hub, Edge, Central
Migration	Azure Migrate, Database Migration Service

Azure Portal, CLI, and PowerShell

Azure offers multiple interfaces to manage resources:

1. Azure Portal

A web-based, graphical interface that allows users to interact with Azure services visually.

2. Azure CLI

A cross-platform command-line tool for managing Azure resources.

Example: Create a resource group

```
az group create --name MyResourceGroup --location westus
```

3. Azure PowerShell

Designed for administrators and script automation in Windows environments.

Example: Create a resource group in PowerShell

```
New-AzResourceGroup -Name "MyResourceGroup" -Location "West US"
```

Azure Resource Hierarchy

Understanding Azure's organizational structure is key to proper governance and scalability.

1. **Management Groups**: Used to manage access, policies, and compliance across multiple subscriptions.

2. **Subscriptions**: Logical containers for billing and resource management.

3. **Resource Groups**: Organize resources by lifecycle or workload.

4. **Resources**: The actual services such as VMs, databases, or storage accounts.

This hierarchy provides flexibility for managing small projects to large enterprise deployments.

Azure Global Reach

Azure spans more than 60+ regions across the globe, each consisting of one or more data centers. Each region provides high availability, redundancy, and data residency compliance.

Key Azure Region Types:

- **Standard Regions**: Full-featured regions for general workloads.

- **Sovereign Regions**: Isolated clouds for government use (e.g., Azure Government).

- **Specialized Regions**: Designed for regulated industries (e.g., Azure China, operated by 21Vianet).

Use the following CLI command to list available regions:

```
az account list-locations --output table
```

Compliance and Security in Azure

Microsoft invests over $1 billion annually in cybersecurity and has more than 3,500 security experts monitoring systems. Azure meets a broad set of international and industry-specific compliance standards, including:

- ISO 27001, 27017, 27018

- GDPR

- HIPAA

- SOC 1, 2, 3

- FedRAMP

- PCI-DSS

Azure also provides compliance offerings via the **Trust Center** and automation through **Azure Policy** and **Blueprints** to enforce configurations across environments.

Free and Trial Services

Azure offers a **free tier** and a **12-month free account** with access to key services such as:

- 750 hours/month of B1S Windows/Linux VM

- 5GB LRS Blob Storage

- 250GB SQL Database (Standard S0)

- 15GB Bandwidth

- Azure Functions and Logic Apps

Use this command to view your current usage:

```
az consumption usage list --top 5 --output table
```

Pricing and Cost Management

Azure provides detailed tools and calculators to manage your costs effectively:

- **Azure Pricing Calculator**: Estimate service costs before deployment.

- **Azure Cost Management**: Analyze and optimize spending.

- **Budgets and Alerts**: Set thresholds and get notified.

Example: Create a budget via CLI

```
az consumption budget create \
  --name MyBudget \
  --amount 100 \
  --time-grain monthly \
  --resource-group MyResourceGroup \
  --time-period start=2025-01-01T00:00:00Z end=2025-12-31T00:00:00Z
```

Azure Ecosystem Integration

Azure integrates seamlessly with the broader Microsoft ecosystem, including:

- **Microsoft 365**

- **Dynamics 365**

- **Visual Studio and GitHub**

- **System Center and Windows Admin Center**

This creates a cohesive development, management, and collaboration environment.

Azure for Developers and IT Pros

For Developers:

- SDKs for .NET, Java, Python, Node.js, Go.

- Visual Studio extensions.

- Azure DevOps for CI/CD pipelines.

- GitHub Actions for workflows.

For IT Professionals:

- Templates for automated infrastructure provisioning (ARM, Bicep, Terraform).

- Azure Monitor, Log Analytics, and Application Insights.

- Policy enforcement with Azure Policy and Defender.

Conclusion

Microsoft Azure is a powerful, enterprise-ready cloud platform that caters to developers, IT professionals, businesses, and government organizations alike. With a massive global footprint, strong integration with Microsoft tools, comprehensive security, and an expansive service catalog, Azure provides a rock-solid foundation for modern cloud architectures.

This section introduced you to Azure's core offerings, organizational structure, deployment interfaces, and key differentiators. As you proceed through the following chapters, you'll dive deeper into configuring and using these services to build real-world solutions. Azure isn't just a cloud — it's an ecosystem of innovation, flexibility, and opportunity.

Azure Global Infrastructure

Microsoft Azure's global infrastructure is the backbone that supports its vast portfolio of cloud services. Spanning across continents and jurisdictions, Azure's infrastructure enables customers to build resilient, low-latency, and globally available applications. It provides unmatched reach, redundancy, compliance, and security, making it one of the most robust public cloud platforms in the world.

This section provides a deep dive into Azure's global architecture, including regions, availability zones, geographies, data centers, edge locations, and connectivity services. You'll also learn how this infrastructure affects your decisions on performance, data residency, compliance, and disaster recovery.

Azure Regions

A **region** in Azure is a set of data centers deployed within a specific geographic area. Each region is designed to provide high availability, redundancy, and fault tolerance.

As of the latest update, Azure has:

- Over **60+ announced regions**

- **200+ physical data centers**

- Presence in **over 140 countries**

Each Azure region is paired with another region within the same geography for **regional pairing**, which ensures data redundancy and disaster recovery support.

Examples of Azure Regions:

- **East US, West US, Central US**

- **North Europe, West Europe**

- **Southeast Asia, East Asia**

- **UK South, UK West**

- **Australia East, Australia Southeast**

To view available regions using CLI:

```
az account list-locations --output table
```

Considerations for Choosing a Region:

- **Data residency** and sovereignty laws.

- **Latency** and proximity to users.

- **Availability of services** (not all services are in every region).

- **Pricing**, which varies by region.

- **Disaster recovery**, using paired regions.

Availability Zones

Availability Zones are physically separate locations within an Azure region. Each zone is made up of one or more data centers equipped with independent power, cooling, and networking. These zones are designed to protect applications and data from data center-level failures.

A region with Availability Zones is referred to as an **AZ-enabled region**.

Key Characteristics:

- Minimum of **three zones per region** for redundancy.

- Synchronous data replication between zones.

- High Availability SLA up to **99.99%** when deploying across zones.

Example Use Case:

Deploy a virtual machine scale set across availability zones to ensure fault tolerance:

```
az vmss create \
  --resource-group MyResourceGroup \
  --name MyScaleSet \
  --image UbuntuLTS \
  --upgrade-policy-mode automatic \
  --zones 1 2 3 \
  --admin-username azureuser \
  --generate-ssh-keys
```

Benefits of Availability Zones:

- Improved **resilience** against data center outages.

- Better **uptime guarantees** for mission-critical apps.

- Ideal for multi-region architecture when combined with regional pairs.

Azure Geographies

An **Azure Geography** is a defined area that contains one or more regions. It is often aligned with geopolitical boundaries and is designed to meet specific **data residency** and **compliance** needs.

Notable Geographies:

- **United States**

- **European Union**

- **United Kingdom**

- **China (operated by 21Vianet)**

- **India**

- **Brazil**

Each geography ensures **data sovereignty** so that data is stored and managed in accordance with applicable regulations, such as:

- **GDPR** in Europe

- **FedRAMP** and **CJIS** in the U.S.

- **IRAP** in Australia

Azure Paired Regions

Every region is paired with another region within the same geography to support:

- **Disaster recovery**

- **Data residency**

- **Automatic replication**

- **Scheduled maintenance alternation**

Azure ensures that updates, such as patches and changes, are rolled out to only one region in a pair at a time, reducing the risk of global outages.

Example of Region Pairings:

Region	Paired Region
East US	West US
North Europe	West Europe
Southeast Asia	East Asia
Japan East	Japan West
Brazil South	South Central US

Data Centers

Azure data centers are highly secure facilities that house the physical servers powering all Azure services. Microsoft builds and maintains its own data centers to ensure full control over:

- **Security**: 24x7 surveillance, biometric access, physical guards.

- **Redundancy**: Power, cooling, and connectivity redundancies.

- **Environmental controls**: Climate regulation and fire suppression.

Each data center is optimized for power efficiency, environmental sustainability, and high-performance computing. Microsoft's carbon-negative goals have driven data center innovations, including underwater data centers and renewable energy sourcing.

Azure Edge Zones and CDN

Azure has expanded its infrastructure with **Edge Zones** and **Content Delivery Network (CDN)** capabilities to serve users closer to where they are.

Azure Edge Zones:

Edge Zones bring compute, storage, and networking closer to end-users to reduce latency for time-sensitive applications like gaming, AR/VR, and real-time analytics.

- **Metro Edge Zones**: Hosted by Microsoft.

- **Carrier Edge Zones**: Deployed with telecom providers (e.g., AT&T, Vodafone).

Azure CDN:

Azure CDN caches content globally, accelerating load times for users anywhere in the world.

```
az cdn endpoint create \
  --resource-group MyCDNGroup \
  --profile-name MyCDNProfile \
  --name MyEndpoint \
  --origin www.mysite.com
```

Global Network and Interconnectivity

Azure boasts one of the largest global networks, featuring:

- **Global backbone network**: Fiber-optic network connecting all regions.

- **Software-defined networking** (SDN) for rapid scaling.

- **ExpressRoute** for private connections.

Azure ExpressRoute:

Provides a private, dedicated connection between on-premises infrastructure and Azure, bypassing the public internet. This results in improved reliability, faster speeds, and enhanced security.

Example: Provisioning ExpressRoute circuit (via portal or ARM templates).

Virtual WAN:

Azure's Virtual WAN simplifies large-scale branch connectivity, allowing businesses to connect offices, data centers, and remote users through SD-WAN or VPN devices.

Service Availability by Region

Not every Azure service is available in every region. Microsoft gradually rolls out services to regions based on demand, compliance, and operational capacity.

To check service availability:

- Visit the Azure Products by Region

- Use the CLI:

```
az vm list-sizes --location "westus2" --output table
```

This helps you plan deployments by verifying whether your desired services and SKUs are offered in a specific region.

Disaster Recovery and Data Replication

Azure's global infrastructure supports advanced business continuity strategies:

- **Geo-Redundant Storage (GRS)**: Automatically replicates data to a paired region.

- **Azure Site Recovery (ASR)**: Enables failover and failback across regions.

- **Zone-Redundant Services**: Some services (e.g., Azure SQL) support built-in zone redundancy.

Example: Enabling GRS for a storage account

```
az storage account create \
  --name mystorageacct \
  --resource-group MyRG \
  --location eastus \
  --sku Standard_GRS
```

Network Latency and Performance

Latency-sensitive applications benefit from deploying in regions closest to end-users. Azure offers:

- **Azure Network Watcher**: Tools to monitor, diagnose, and view metrics.

- **Traffic Manager**: DNS-based load balancing for global applications.

You can measure latency using the **Azure Speed Test** tool or perform manual tests using:

```
ping <region-specific-endpoint>
```

Or for more comprehensive results:

```
az network watcher test-connectivity \
  --source-resource <VMName> \
  --dest-address <destination IP> \
  --dest-port 443
```

Compliance and Data Residency

Each Azure region adheres to specific compliance standards. Microsoft maintains the **Azure Compliance Manager** to help businesses meet regulatory obligations.

You can choose regions based on:

- **Data location laws**

- **Industry compliance requirements**

- **Customer or internal policy**

For example, deploying in **Germany West Central** ensures data does not leave German jurisdiction — a critical consideration for financial or healthcare institutions.

Conclusion

Microsoft Azure's global infrastructure is unparalleled in its reach, resilience, and compliance coverage. With strategically placed regions, availability zones, and edge zones, Azure enables the creation of high-performance, low-latency, and globally distributed applications.

Key takeaways:

- Azure regions and zones ensure business continuity and fault tolerance.

- Geographies and regional pairings address legal and regulatory needs.

- Tools like ExpressRoute and Azure CDN reduce latency and improve user experience.

- Microsoft's sustainability and innovation efforts make Azure a future-ready platform.

Understanding Azure's infrastructure is crucial when architecting applications, selecting deployment strategies, and ensuring regulatory compliance. This foundation supports all services explored in later chapters and is essential for cloud solution architects, developers, and administrators alike.

Creating Your First Azure Account

Before you can start deploying virtual machines, building web apps, or storing data in Microsoft Azure, you need to create an Azure account. This section will walk you through the entire process of creating a Microsoft Azure account, including setting up a free subscription, verifying your identity, understanding account structures, managing permissions, and configuring essential settings to ensure a smooth and secure start.

Creating your Azure account is more than just filling in a few details—it's about laying the groundwork for effective and secure cloud usage. We'll cover the necessary steps, best practices, and considerations so you can begin your Azure journey confidently.

Step 1: Visit the Azure Signup Portal

To get started with Microsoft Azure, navigate to the official sign-up page:

https://azure.microsoft.com/free

This page will give you access to a **12-month free tier**, a **30-day $200 credit**, and **always-free services** such as:

- 750 hours/month of B1S virtual machine

- 5 GB of Blob storage

- 250 GB of SQL Database (S0 tier)

- 15 GB of outbound data transfer

- 1 million Azure Function executions

Click **Start free** to begin the signup process.

Step 2: Sign In or Create a Microsoft Account

You will be prompted to sign in with a Microsoft account. If you already use Outlook, Xbox Live, or Office 365, you likely have a Microsoft account.

If you don't, click **Create one!** to register a new Microsoft account. You'll need to provide:

- A valid email address

- Password

- Country/region

- Date of birth

After creating the account, verify your email and proceed to the Azure registration.

Step 3: Identity Verification and Payment Information

To prevent abuse of free resources, Microsoft requires users to verify their identity with:

1. **Phone Verification**:

   - Choose your country code.

   - Receive a verification code via SMS or voice call.

2. **Credit or Debit Card Verification**:

   - Enter valid payment information (Visa, Mastercard, American Express).

   - Microsoft will place a temporary authorization (usually $1) to confirm the card's validity.

Note: Microsoft does **not** charge you during the trial unless you explicitly upgrade your subscription. You can use the portal to monitor usage and billing at any time.

Step 4: Choose Your Subscription Type

After verification, you'll be prompted to choose a subscription. During the trial period, you are automatically placed on the **Azure Free Trial** subscription.

Azure supports several subscription types:

Subscription Type	Description
Free Trial	$200 credit for 30 days, 12-month free limited services
Pay-As-You-Go	Billed monthly for services consumed
Enterprise Agreement	Large-volume licensing for organizations
Microsoft Customer Agreement	Used by large-scale organizations with multiple tenants
Student Account	No credit card needed; includes free services for learning

Step 5: Accept the Terms and Complete Setup

Review and accept Microsoft's **subscription agreement**, **offer details**, and **privacy statement**. Once accepted, you will be redirected to the **Azure Portal**.

Congratulations! Your Azure account is now active, and your journey into the Microsoft Cloud has officially begun.

Navigating the Azure Portal

The Azure Portal is the web-based interface for managing your Azure resources. After logging in at https://portal.azure.com, you'll be presented with the **Azure Dashboard**.

Key sections of the portal include:

- **Home**: Overview of recent resources and quick start guides.

- **Dashboard**: Customizable canvas with pinned resources.

- **All Services**: Full list of Azure services.

- **Resource Groups**: Logical containers for resources.

- **Subscriptions**: Manage billing and quotas.

You can customize your dashboard with tiles, charts, and pinned services for easier access.

Understanding Azure Account Structure

Azure has a **hierarchical account structure** that supports governance, billing, and resource organization.

1. Microsoft Account / Work Account

This is the identity used to sign into Azure. It can be:

- A **personal Microsoft account** (e.g., john.doe@outlook.com)

- An **Azure Active Directory (AAD) account** used in enterprise settings

2. Azure Subscription

A subscription is the **billing boundary**. Each subscription can have:

- Quotas and usage limits

- Payment methods and billing history

- Resource groups and services

- Role-based access control (RBAC)

You can create multiple subscriptions under a single account to separate projects, environments, or teams.

3. Resource Groups

A resource group is a **logical container** for Azure resources. Use them to manage access, policies, and lifecycles.

4. Resources

These are the actual services like virtual machines, storage accounts, databases, and web apps.

Role-Based Access Control (RBAC)

When collaborating with a team, use RBAC to assign **fine-grained permissions**.

Azure provides built-in roles:

- **Owner**: Full control including access management

- **Contributor**: Can manage resources but not access

- **Reader**: Can view but not change resources

You can assign roles at different scopes:

- Management Group

- Subscription

- Resource Group

- Individual Resource

```
az role assignment create \
  --assignee <user-email> \
  --role Contributor \
  --resource-group MyResourceGroup
```

This command assigns the Contributor role to a user for a specific resource group.

Setting Up MFA and Security Alerts

Securing your Azure account is critical. After account creation, you should:

1. **Enable Multi-Factor Authentication (MFA)**:
   Enforce MFA on your Microsoft or AAD account to prevent unauthorized access.

2. **Review Sign-In Activity**:
   Check the Azure AD blade to audit logins and set alerts for suspicious activity.

3. **Activate Security Center**:
   Use Microsoft Defender for Cloud to monitor and secure your environment.

Azure CLI and PowerShell Setup

For automation and scripting, install the Azure CLI or Azure PowerShell:

Azure CLI (cross-platform):
```
curl -sL https://aka.ms/InstallAzureCLIDeb | sudo bash
az login
```

Azure PowerShell (Windows/macOS/Linux):
```
Install-Module -Name Az -AllowClobber -Scope CurrentUser
Connect-AzAccount
```

These tools provide programmatic access to create, manage, and monitor Azure services.

Monitoring Your Trial Usage

Keep track of your $200 credit and free tier usage via:

1. **Azure Portal → Cost Management + Billing**

2. **Set up Budget Alerts**

3. **Download Usage Reports**

You can also use this CLI command to view your current usage:

```
az consumption usage list --output table
```

Once your trial ends or credit is used, services are paused, and you can choose to upgrade to Pay-As-You-Go.

Converting to a Paid Subscription

When ready to move beyond the trial:

1. Go to **Subscriptions** in the Azure Portal

2. Select your trial subscription

3. Click **Upgrade**

4. Confirm your billing information

All your resources will continue to function seamlessly under the new billing model.

Best Practices for New Accounts

- **Use Resource Tags** to categorize usage (e.g., Environment=Dev, Owner=JohnDoe).

- **Create Multiple Subscriptions** for Dev/Test vs. Production environments.

- **Limit Owner Roles** to a few trusted accounts.

- **Audit Access Logs** regularly.

- **Review Azure Advisor** for optimization suggestions.

Conclusion

Creating your first Azure account is a crucial and exciting step into the cloud. It's not just about signing up — it's about laying the foundation for secure, scalable, and manageable cloud adoption.

From understanding subscriptions and account structure to enabling security features and navigating the portal, this section has guided you through everything needed to get started. Whether you're experimenting with free services or preparing for enterprise-scale deployments, your Azure account is the gateway to a world of cloud innovation.

As we continue through the book, you'll use this account to provision resources, deploy applications, and explore Azure services in depth. Be sure to familiarize yourself with the portal and tools — they'll be essential in your journey.

Navigating the Azure Portal

Once your Azure account is created and active, the Azure Portal becomes your central hub for managing cloud services, monitoring resource health, deploying applications, and configuring policies. The Azure Portal provides a powerful web-based graphical interface to interact with every aspect of your cloud infrastructure, whether you're deploying virtual machines, configuring networking, analyzing usage metrics, or setting up automation.

This section provides a comprehensive walkthrough of the Azure Portal, covering its layout, major components, customization options, resource management tools, integrated services, and tips for boosting your productivity. You will also learn how to locate services, use the command palette, and optimize your dashboard for various roles, such as developers, system administrators, or architects.

Azure Portal Overview

The Azure Portal is available at:

https://portal.azure.com

It is a fully responsive web application that works across desktops, laptops, and tablets. You sign in using your Microsoft or organizational account to access the resources linked to your subscriptions.

The Portal's interface is highly dynamic, with flyout panels and customizable dashboards, offering powerful visualization and drill-down capabilities. You can manage all aspects of your cloud environment without needing to install tools or use the command line.

Portal Layout and Main Components

Understanding the portal's layout is essential for effective navigation. Key components include:

1. Global Search Bar

Located at the top, the global search bar allows you to find:

- Resources (VMs, storage, databases)

- Resource groups and subscriptions

- Services (App Services, Cosmos DB, etc.)

- Documentation and marketplace items

This feature uses intelligent suggestions based on usage patterns and provides quick access to almost anything in Azure.

2. Navigation Menu (Left Panel)

This collapsible panel gives access to frequently used features:

- **Home**

- **Dashboard**

- **All Services**

- **Resource Groups**

- **Subscriptions**

- **Marketplace**

- **Azure Active Directory**

- **Cost Management**

- **Help + Support**

You can pin or unpin services for faster access based on your workflow.

3. Dashboard

The Dashboard is a customizable landing page where you can pin and arrange tiles representing resources, charts, shortcuts, and service health.

- Create multiple dashboards per role, project, or team.

- Use visualizations like metrics, alerts, usage graphs.

- Clone and share dashboards with others in your organization.

4. Notifications Pane

This bell icon alerts you about:

- Resource deployment status

- Recommendations

- Billing updates

- Security alerts

Click any notification to see detailed logs or troubleshoot.

5. Cloud Shell and Command Palette

- **Cloud Shell**: Integrated terminal supporting Bash and PowerShell. Access CLI tools without installing anything locally.

- **Command Palette (Ctrl + /)**: Fast-access tool similar to command palettes in IDEs, allowing you to execute actions like "Create VM" or "Open Logs" by typing.

Finding and Using Services

There are three primary ways to find Azure services in the portal:

1. Search Bar

Type a keyword like "Storage" or "Function App," and click the desired service.

2. All Services

Access the full catalog of Azure offerings, categorized by function:

- Compute

- Networking

- Databases

- AI + Machine Learning

- Internet of Things

- DevOps

- Monitoring

Filter by category, tag favorites, and sort alphabetically.

3. Marketplace

Explore third-party and Microsoft-certified solutions, including:

- Virtual appliances

- Preconfigured VMs

- SaaS applications

- Automation templates

Example: Launching a VM from the portal

1. Go to "Virtual Machines"

2. Click "+ Create"

3. Select "Azure virtual machine"

4. Fill in configuration details: name, region, image (Ubuntu, Windows), size

5. Review + Create → Launch

Resource Groups and Tagging

Azure resources are grouped into **Resource Groups**, which act as containers for logically associated services.

Resource Group Features:

- Shared lifecycle (delete a group to remove all its contents)

- Unified access controls

- Easier cost tracking and automation

You can create a resource group directly from the portal:

1. Click "Resource groups" → "+ Create"

2. Enter name and region

3. Tag appropriately (Environment = Dev, Project = Website)

Tagging enhances resource management by assigning metadata to items. Use consistent naming conventions and tags for easier billing, automation, and policy enforcement.

Example tags:

Name	Value

Environment	Production
Owner	Alice Johnson
CostCenter	1234

Working with Resources

Each resource in Azure has a **blade** (panel) showing details, metrics, and management options. Common elements:

- **Overview**: Status, location, resource ID
- **Monitoring**: CPU, memory, network, logs
- **Access control**: RBAC assignments
- **Configuration**: Settings like size, IP address, firewall rules
- **Activity Log**: Audit trail of changes

You can perform actions such as:

- Start/stop VMs
- Scale up/down
- View connection strings
- Export templates (ARM, Bicep)
- Lock resources to prevent accidental deletion

Deploying Resources with Templates

Azure supports Infrastructure as Code (IaC) using ARM templates and Bicep. From the portal:

1. Select "Deploy a custom template"

2. Use pre-defined templates from Quickstart Gallery or write your own

3. Fill in parameters and deploy

This method standardizes deployment and simplifies environment replication.

Example ARM deployment via portal:

```json
{
  "$schema": "https://schema.management.azure.com/schemas/2019-04-01/deploymentTemplate.json#",
  "contentVersion": "1.0.0.0",
  "resources": [
    {
      "type": "Microsoft.Storage/storageAccounts",
      "apiVersion": "2021-04-01",
      "name": "mystorageacct123",
      "location": "eastus",
      "sku": {
        "name": "Standard_LRS"
      },
      "kind": "StorageV2",
      "properties": {}
    }
  ]
}
```

Monitoring and Insights

The Azure Portal integrates deeply with monitoring and diagnostics tools:

- **Azure Monitor**: Centralized platform for logs, metrics, alerts.

- **Application Insights**: End-to-end monitoring for applications.

- **Log Analytics**: Kusto Query Language (KQL)-based log querying.

Example: View performance metrics for a VM

1. Go to Virtual Machine → Monitoring → Metrics

2. Choose metric (e.g., CPU percentage)

3. Set time range, granularity, and visualization type

You can create alerts from these charts to notify you of threshold breaches (e.g., CPU > 80%).

Cost Analysis and Billing

From the portal, go to **Cost Management + Billing** to:

- View current spend

- Forecast future costs

- Download usage reports

- Set budget alerts

Use the cost analysis blade to break down usage by service, resource group, or tag.

To set a budget alert:

1. Go to "Cost Management" → "Budgets" → "+ Add"

2. Define name, amount, reset period

3. Add recipients for alert notifications

Productivity Tips

- **Pin to Dashboard**: Any resource or blade can be pinned for easy access.

- **Dark Mode**: Switch themes for a more comfortable viewing experience.

- **Keyboard Shortcuts**:

    o / → Focus search bar

- ○ g + d → Go to dashboard

- ○ ? → View all shortcuts

- **Shareable URLs**: Copy the direct link to a resource for team collaboration.

- **Global Filters**: Filter views by subscription, region, or resource group across the entire portal.

Managing Access with Azure Active Directory

Navigate to **Azure Active Directory** in the portal to:

- View and manage users, groups, and roles

- Configure enterprise apps and single sign-on (SSO)

- Apply conditional access policies

- Enable MFA for accounts

Admins can create custom roles and assign them via RBAC at the subscription or resource level.

Troubleshooting and Support

Azure Portal integrates with support tools for issue resolution:

- **Help + Support**: Create a new support request

- **Diagnose and solve problems**: Automated troubleshooting suggestions

- **Service Health**: Track outages and maintenance events in your region

Microsoft also offers chat and email support through the portal, with faster response times depending on your support plan.

Conclusion

The Azure Portal is a robust, user-friendly interface that centralizes everything you need to deploy, monitor, and manage your cloud services. From the moment you log in, you have full control over infrastructure, applications, identity, security, and billing—all from a single web portal.

By mastering navigation, dashboards, templates, tagging, and monitoring tools, you can dramatically improve your productivity and operational control. As you progress through more advanced topics in this book, the portal will serve as both a teaching aid and a control center for hands-on learning and experimentation.

Understanding Azure Subscriptions and Resource Groups

Azure provides a highly flexible, scalable, and organized way to manage your cloud resources. To achieve this, it uses a logical hierarchy that starts with **subscriptions** and **resource groups**, which serve as the foundation for structuring, organizing, and governing your cloud environment.

This section will guide you through the core concepts of Azure subscriptions and resource groups, how they interact, their best practices, and how to manage them effectively using both the Azure Portal and command-line tools. Understanding these building blocks is crucial for setting up a well-governed, cost-effective, and secure Azure architecture, especially in multi-user or enterprise environments.

What Is an Azure Subscription?

An **Azure subscription** is essentially a container that holds a collection of Azure resources. It defines:

- **Billing boundaries**: Costs are calculated and charged at the subscription level.

- **Access controls**: Permissions and role-based access are scoped per subscription.

- **Service quotas and limits**: Azure enforces usage limits per subscription (e.g., number of vCPUs, storage accounts).

Each Azure account can contain **multiple subscriptions**. This is particularly useful for:

- Separating environments (e.g., Development, Testing, Production)

- Isolating business units or projects

- Applying different billing or cost center tracking

- Managing access and compliance boundaries

Subscription Types

Azure offers several types of subscriptions to accommodate different scenarios:

Subscription Type	Description
Free Trial	$200 credit for 30 days + 12-month free services
Pay-As-You-Go	No upfront cost, billed monthly based on usage
Microsoft Customer Agreement	Used for enterprise-level agreements and consolidated billing
Enterprise Agreement	Volume licensing for large-scale organizations
Student	Free services for verified students, no credit card required
Sponsorship	Custom-funded or grant-based subscriptions

To view your current subscription(s) in the portal; go to:

Azure Portal → Subscriptions

Or via CLI:

```
az account list --output table
```

To set a default subscription:

```
az account set --subscription "Your Subscription Name"
```

Subscription Hierarchy and Management Groups

For organizations with many subscriptions, Azure provides a higher-level container called **Management Groups**. These allow you to:

- Apply policies and RBAC across multiple subscriptions

- Create hierarchical structures (e.g., Organization > Department > Team)

- Simplify compliance and cost management

Hierarchy Example:

```
Management Group: ContosoRoot
|
|── Management Group: IT
|   |── Subscription: DevOps
|   └── Subscription: QA
|
└── Management Group: Finance
    └── Subscription: AccountingApp
```

To create a management group using Azure CLI:

```
az account management-group create --name FinanceGroup --display-
name "Finance Department"
```

What Is a Resource Group?

A **Resource Group (RG)** is a container that holds related Azure resources. These can include:

- Virtual machines

- Storage accounts

- Databases

- Network interfaces

- App services

Resource groups enable centralized management of resources that share a lifecycle or purpose. For example, a web application and its associated database and load balancer can all live in one RG.

Key Characteristics:

- **Single region scope for metadata**, but resources can span multiple regions.

- **Lifecycle management**: Deleting a resource group deletes all included resources.

- **RBAC scope**: Permissions can be scoped to individual resource groups.

- **Tagging and cost analysis**: Tags applied at RG level propagate to included resources.

Creating and Managing Resource Groups

You can create a resource group in multiple ways:

Azure Portal:

1. Navigate to "Resource groups"

2. Click "+ Create"

3. Provide name and region

4. Click "Review + Create"

Azure CLI:

```
az group create --name MyResourceGroup --location eastus
```

To view all resource groups:

```
az group list --output table
```

To delete a resource group:

```
az group delete --name MyResourceGroup --yes --no-wait
```

This command deletes the RG and all resources inside it — use with caution.

Resource Group Best Practices

1. **Group by Lifecycle**: Keep resources that are created, modified, and deleted together in the same RG.

2. **Use Naming Conventions**: Define a consistent naming scheme for RGs (e.g., `rg-webapp-prod`, `rg-db-dev`).

3. **Apply Tags**: Use tags like `Owner`, `Environment`, `CostCenter`, `Department`.

4. **Avoid Cross-Environment Sharing**: Don't place dev and prod resources in the same RG.

5. **Lock Important RGs**: Prevent accidental deletion using resource locks.

Example tag application:

```
az tag create --resource-id
/subscriptions/{subId}/resourceGroups/MyResourceGroup \
--tags Environment=Production Department=Finance Owner=JohnDoe
```

Tagging Resources and Groups

Tags are key-value pairs attached to resources or resource groups to organize and track resources.

Benefits of Tagging:

- Simplifies cost tracking across departments or projects

- Enables automation via policies

- Improves searchability and reporting

- Helps enforce governance

Example Tag Structure:

Key	Value
Environment	Development
Owner	SarahConnor

Project	CRMSystem
CostCenter	4567

Tags can be added during or after resource creation. You can also enforce tagging through **Azure Policy**.

RBAC at Subscription and RG Level

Role-Based Access Control (RBAC) can be scoped at:

- **Subscription level**: Users get access to all RGs and resources.

- **Resource Group level**: Users access only the specified group.

- **Resource level**: Granular control (e.g., can manage VMs but not databases).

Example: Assign "Reader" role at RG level via CLI:

```
az role assignment create \
  --assignee john.doe@example.com \
  --role Reader \
  --resource-group FinanceRG
```

This ensures John Doe can view but not modify resources in the FinanceRG.

Subscription-Level Quotas and Limits

Each subscription has limits that affect the number of resources you can deploy. Examples:

Resource Type	Default Limit
Virtual Machines	10 per region
Storage Accounts	250 per region
Public IP Addresses	20 per region

VNETs   50 per region

These can be increased by submitting a **quota request** via the portal:

1. Go to "Subscriptions"

2. Select your subscription

3. Click "Usage + quotas"

4. Request increase

Billing and Cost Management by Subscription

Each subscription has its own billing cycle and invoice. You can:

- Set **budgets**

- Analyze **spending trends**

- Break down costs by **service**, **tag**, or **resource group**

To view current cost:

```
az consumption usage list --subscription "MySubName" --output table
```

To create a budget:

```
az consumption budget create \
  --name ITBudget \
  --amount 500 \
  --time-grain monthly \
  --resource-group ITGroup \
  --time-period start=2025-01-01T00:00:00Z end=2025-12-31T00:00:00Z
```

Azure Policy and Governance

Azure Policy helps enforce organizational standards across subscriptions and RGs.

Examples:

- Require tags on all resources

- Deny creation of certain VM sizes

- Enforce location compliance (e.g., only deploy in UK South)

Create a policy using the portal or CLI and assign it to a scope (subscription or RG).

Example: Require a specific tag

```
az policy definition create \
  --name require-env-tag \
  --rules 'policy-rules.json' \
  --display-name "Require Environment Tag" \
  --mode All
```

Migrating Resources Between RGs and Subscriptions

Azure supports moving resources between:

- Resource Groups within the same subscription

- Subscriptions (with limitations)

To move resources:

1. Select the resource in the portal

2. Click "Move" → "Move to another resource group"

3. Select destination RG or subscription

Or via CLI:

```
az resource move \
  --destination-group NewRG \
  --ids
/subscriptions/{subId}/resourceGroups/OldRG/providers/Microsoft.Comp
ute/virtualMachines/MyVM
```

Ensure dependent resources are moved together to avoid errors.

Conclusion

Understanding Azure subscriptions and resource groups is critical for maintaining a well-organized, cost-effective, and secure cloud environment. These components act as the administrative, billing, and management backbone of all Azure activity.

By strategically creating subscriptions and organizing resources into logical resource groups, you can:

- Improve visibility and control

- Simplify access management

- Track and reduce costs

- Enforce compliance policies

- Enable automation and scalability

As you continue your journey in Azure, these foundational concepts will shape the way you architect, secure, and optimize your solutions in the cloud.

Chapter 3: Core Azure Services Explained

Compute: Azure Virtual Machines and App Services

In the world of cloud computing, compute services form the backbone of most applications and services. Microsoft Azure offers a wide range of compute services designed to meet diverse needs—from full control of virtual machines (VMs) to simplified deployment using platform-as-a-service (PaaS) options like Azure App Services. Understanding these services is essential for any developer, system administrator, or architect working with Azure.

Introduction to Azure Compute

Azure Compute is a suite of services that provide the infrastructure and tools required to run applications on the cloud. These services include virtual machines, container services, and web applications. Azure allows you to scale from a single instance to thousands depending on your needs, all managed through a unified platform.

The two most widely used compute services in Azure are:

- **Azure Virtual Machines (VMs)**: Infrastructure-as-a-Service (IaaS) offering full control over the OS and environment.

- **Azure App Services**: Platform-as-a-Service (PaaS) offering for deploying web applications with minimal management overhead.

Let's explore these in depth.

Azure Virtual Machines

Azure VMs allow users to deploy and manage virtualized Windows or Linux servers. This is the go-to option when you need full control over your development environment, software stack, and custom configurations.

Key Features

- **Custom Operating System**: Choose from a wide variety of preconfigured images or upload your own.

- **High Availability**: Use Availability Sets and Zones to ensure uptime.

- **Scalability**: Scale sets allow you to run thousands of identical VMs.

- **Integrated Monitoring**: Azure Monitor and Log Analytics provide visibility into performance and usage.

Creating an Azure Virtual Machine

To create an Azure VM using the Azure Portal:

1. Sign in to the Azure Portal.

2. Navigate to **Virtual Machines** > **Create** > **Virtual Machine**.

3. Fill out the basic settings including subscription, resource group, and VM details.

4. Select the image (e.g., Ubuntu, Windows Server).

5. Choose an appropriate size (based on vCPU, RAM).

6. Set up authentication (password or SSH key).

7. Configure networking options (Virtual Network, Subnet, Public IP).

8. Review and create the VM.

Using Azure CLI

Here's how to create a VM using the Azure CLI:

```
az vm create \
  --resource-group MyResourceGroup \
  --name MyVM \
  --image UbuntuLTS \
  --admin-username azureuser \
  --generate-ssh-keys
```

This command provisions a VM named MyVM using the latest Ubuntu image.

Azure App Services

Azure App Services is a fully managed platform for building, deploying, and scaling web apps. It supports multiple programming languages including .NET, Node.js, Java, Python, and PHP.

Key Features

- **Integrated Tools**: Built-in CI/CD via GitHub, Azure DevOps, and Docker Hub.

- **Auto Scaling**: Automatically adjusts resources based on demand.

- **Custom Domains & SSL**: Easily bind custom domains with free or custom SSL certificates.

- **Staging Environments**: Use slots for blue-green deployments.

Creating a Web App with Azure Portal

1. Go to **App Services** > **Create**.

2. Select a **Resource Group** and enter the app name.

3. Choose the **Runtime stack** and **Region**.

4. Select an appropriate **App Service Plan** based on your scaling needs.

5. Review and create.

Once deployed, you can push code directly via Git or deploy using FTP.

Using Azure CLI

You can also deploy a web app using the Azure CLI:

```
az webapp up \
  --name MyWebApp \
  --resource-group MyResourceGroup \
  --location westeurope
```

This command creates and deploys a basic web app using the current directory as the code base.

Choosing Between Azure VMs and App Services

Feature	Azure VMs	Azure App Services
Control	Full OS-level control	Limited to app-level configuration
Management Overhead	High	Low

Scaling	Manual or auto with scale sets	Automatic
Use Case	Custom environments, legacy apps	Web apps, APIs, microservices

Use Azure VMs when you need to install custom software, run background processes, or have specific OS configurations.
 Use Azure App Services when you need fast deployment with built-in scalability and lower maintenance.

Advanced Concepts

Virtual Machine Scale Sets

Scale sets allow you to deploy and manage a set of identical, load-balanced VMs. They are ideal for high availability and scalability.

```
az vmss create \
  --resource-group MyResourceGroup \
  --name MyScaleSet \
  --image UbuntuLTS \
  --upgrade-policy-mode automatic \
  --admin-username azureuser \
  --generate-ssh-keys
```

Deployment Slots in App Services

Deployment slots in App Services allow you to stage your app in a separate environment before swapping it into production. This helps with safe rollouts and testing.

```
az webapp deployment slot create \
  --name MyWebApp \
  --resource-group MyResourceGroup \
  --slot staging
```

You can then deploy to the `staging` slot and swap when ready:

```
az webapp deployment slot swap \
  --name MyWebApp \
  --resource-group MyResourceGroup \
  --slot staging
```

Monitoring and Performance

Azure provides built-in tools to monitor the performance of both VMs and App Services.

For VMs

- **Azure Monitor**: Collect metrics and logs.

- **Log Analytics**: Run queries against collected data.

- **Azure Advisor**: Provides performance and cost recommendations.

For App Services

- **App Insights**: Track request rates, response times, failures.

- **Diagnostics Logs**: Capture system-level logs and errors.

```
az monitor diagnostic-settings create \
  --resource
"/subscriptions/xxx/resourceGroups/MyResourceGroup/providers/Microso
ft.Web/sites/MyWebApp" \
  --name "myDiagnosticSetting" \
  --workspace "<LogAnalyticsWorkspaceID>" \
  --logs '[{"category":"AppServiceHTTPLogs","enabled":true}]'
```

Security Considerations

- For **VMs**, ensure SSH ports are not open to the internet unless necessary.

- Use **Network Security Groups (NSGs)** and **Just-In-Time VM Access** for additional protection.

- For **App Services**, enforce HTTPS and use Azure Key Vault to manage secrets securely.

Best Practices

- **Start with App Services** unless your use case specifically requires VMs.

- **Automate deployments** using GitHub Actions, Azure DevOps, or Bicep/ARM templates.

- **Tag resources** for cost tracking and lifecycle management.

- **Back up regularly** using Azure Backup or snapshots.

- **Monitor everything**: performance, errors, and costs.

Conclusion

Azure's compute services offer both flexibility and power. Whether you're deploying a highly customized environment with Azure Virtual Machines or a scalable web application with App Services, Azure provides the tools and infrastructure to meet your needs. By mastering these services, you lay a solid foundation for more advanced cloud solutions including containers, serverless, and DevOps automation.

In the next sections, we'll explore other core services in Azure such as storage, networking, and databases, which integrate tightly with the compute layer to form a complete cloud ecosystem.

Storage: Blob, Disk, and File Storage

Azure offers a rich set of cloud storage solutions designed for reliability, scalability, and security. These solutions cater to diverse workloads—whether you're dealing with unstructured data, virtual machine disks, or shared files for enterprise applications. Understanding Azure Storage is essential for building robust, scalable applications that can handle massive data volumes efficiently.

This section delves deep into the core Azure storage offerings:

- **Azure Blob Storage** (object storage for unstructured data)

- **Azure Disk Storage** (block storage for virtual machines)

- **Azure Files** (managed file shares)

Azure Storage Overview

Azure Storage is Microsoft's cloud storage solution for modern data storage scenarios. It offers high durability (99.999999999%, or "11 nines"), strong consistency, low latency, and comprehensive security features like encryption and role-based access control.

Core capabilities include:

- **Redundancy**: Options like LRS, ZRS, GRS ensure data durability.

- **Scalability**: Petabytes of data supported per account.

- **Security**: Data encryption at rest and in transit, integration with Azure AD.

- **Accessibility**: REST APIs, SDKs, Azure CLI, PowerShell, and Portal access.

Each type of storage service is optimized for specific use cases.

Azure Blob Storage

Azure Blob Storage is Microsoft's object storage solution for the cloud. It is optimized for storing massive amounts of unstructured data such as images, videos, audio, logs, backups, and big data workloads.

Blob Types

1. **Block Blobs** – Store text and binary data. Ideal for documents, media files.

2. **Append Blobs** – Optimized for append operations, great for logs.

3. **Page Blobs** – Used primarily for virtual hard disks (VHDs).

Storage Tiers

- **Hot** – Frequently accessed data; higher cost, low latency.

- **Cool** – Infrequently accessed data; lower cost, slightly higher latency.

- **Archive** – Rarely accessed data; very low cost, high latency for retrieval.

Creating a Blob Storage Container

Using Azure CLI:

```
# Create a resource group
az group create --name storage-rg --location eastus

# Create a storage account
az storage account create --name mystorageaccount --resource-group
storage-rg --location eastus --sku Standard_LRS
```

```
# Create a blob container
az storage container create --name mycontainer --account-name
mystorageaccount --public-access off
```

Uploading a File
```
az storage blob upload \
  --account-name mystorageaccount \
  --container-name mycontainer \
  --name myfile.txt \
  --file ./myfile.txt
```

Access Control

- Use **SAS tokens** for secure time-limited access.
- Integrate with **Azure Active Directory** for granular RBAC.

Common Use Cases

- Serving images, documents, or videos
- Backup and disaster recovery
- Big data analytics (with Azure Data Lake integration)
- Archive storage

Azure Disk Storage

Azure Disk Storage provides high-performance, durable block storage for Azure Virtual Machines. It is ideal for workloads requiring consistent performance and low latency, such as databases and critical business applications.

Disk Types

1. **Premium SSD** – High-performance, low-latency disks for IO-intensive workloads.
2. **Standard SSD** – Cost-effective SSD option for moderate performance needs.
3. **Standard HDD** – Economical disks for infrequent access and testing.

4. **Ultra Disks** – Extreme performance, customizable IOPS and throughput.

Attaching a Disk to a VM

```
az disk create \
  --resource-group myResourceGroup \
  --name myDataDisk \
  --size-gb 128 \
  --sku Premium_LRS

az vm disk attach \
  --vm-name myVM \
  --resource-group myResourceGroup \
  --name myDataDisk
```

Snapshot and Backup

Azure supports point-in-time snapshots for data protection and incremental backups for efficient disaster recovery.

```
az snapshot create \
  --resource-group myResourceGroup \
  --source myDataDisk \
  --name mySnapshot
```

Performance Tiers

Disks come with performance metrics like:

- IOPS (Input/Output Operations Per Second)

- Throughput (MB/sec)

You can dynamically change the performance tier on Premium SSDs without downtime.

Azure Files

Azure Files offers fully managed file shares in the cloud, accessible via SMB and NFS protocols. These shares can be mounted on Windows, macOS, and Linux systems, both in the cloud and on-premises using Azure File Sync.

Key Features

- **SMB 3.0 & NFS 4.1 Support**

- **Snapshot-Based Backups**

- **Integration with AD DS and Azure AD**

- **Geo-Redundant Storage**

Creating an Azure File Share

```
az storage share create \
  --account-name mystorageaccount \
  --name myfileshare
```

Mounting the Share (Windows Example)

```
# From a Windows machine
net use Z: \\mystorageaccount.file.core.windows.net\myfileshare
/u:mystorageaccount <storage_key>
```

For Linux:

```
sudo mount -t cifs
//mystorageaccount.file.core.windows.net/myfileshare /mnt/myshare -o
vers=3.0,username=mystorageaccount,password=<storage_key>,dir_mode=0
777,file_mode=0777
```

Azure File Sync

Azure File Sync enables centralization of your organization's file shares in Azure Files, while keeping the flexibility and performance of a local file server.

Use Case: If you have multiple branch offices with local file servers, use Azure File Sync to keep all locations in sync with the cloud, and offload cold files automatically.

Comparing Blob, Disk, and File Storage

Feature	Blob Storage	Disk Storage	File Storage
Access Pattern	REST APIs, SDKs	Attached to VMs	SMB/NFS mounts

Best for	Unstructured data	VM disks, databases	Shared drives, lift & shift
Performance	High for Hot tier	Consistent, high	Medium
Mountable	No	Yes (VM-only)	Yes (multi-platform)
Backup & Recovery	Snapshots, Archive	Snapshots	Snapshots, File Sync
Protocol	HTTPS	Block-level I/O	SMB, NFS

Security and Compliance

Azure Storage is highly secure and supports:

- **Encryption at Rest**: All data is encrypted using Microsoft-managed or customer-managed keys in Azure Key Vault.

- **TLS in Transit**: Enforced HTTPS connections.

- **RBAC & IAM**: Integrates with Azure AD for granular control.

- **Private Endpoints**: Connect storage securely over a private IP within your VNet.

- **Advanced Threat Protection**: Alerts for unusual access patterns.

```
az storage account update \
  --name mystorageaccount \
  --resource-group storage-rg \
  --default-action Deny \
  --enable-hierarchical-namespace true
```

Monitoring and Diagnostics

Azure provides various tools to monitor and diagnose storage usage:

- **Azure Monitor**: Collects and visualizes metrics like capacity, latency, and request rates.

- **Diagnostic Logs**: Include read/write operations, latency, and errors.

- **Alerts**: Set thresholds for usage, capacity, or anomaly detection.

```
az monitor metrics alert create \
  --name HighBlobLatency \
  --resource-group storage-rg \
  --scopes "/subscriptions/.../storageAccounts/mystorageaccount" \
  --condition "avg SuccessE2ELatency > 200" \
  --description "Alert when latency exceeds 200ms"
```

Best Practices

- **Choose the right tier**: Align storage tiers with data access patterns to optimize cost.

- **Use lifecycle management policies** to automatically transition blobs between tiers.

- **Encrypt sensitive data** with customer-managed keys when needed.

- **Implement redundancy** based on criticality: LRS for dev/test, GRS/ZRS for production.

- **Tag your storage resources** for better governance and billing insights.

```
az storage account management-policy create \
  --account-name mystorageaccount \
  --resource-group storage-rg \
  --policy @policy.json
```

Example `policy.json`:

```json
{
  "rules": [
    {
      "name": "archive-inactive",
      "enabled": true,
      "definition": {
        "filters": {
          "blobTypes": [ "blockBlob" ]
        },
        "actions": {
          "baseBlob": {
```

```
        "tierToCool": {
          "daysAfterModificationGreaterThan": 30
        },
        "tierToArchive": {
          "daysAfterModificationGreaterThan": 90
        }
      }
    }
   }
  }
 ]
}
```

Conclusion

Azure's storage offerings are built to support modern enterprise and cloud-native applications at scale. Whether you need massive object storage, high-performance disks, or shared file access, Azure provides a comprehensive suite of options. Mastery of Blob, Disk, and File Storage services is foundational for architects, developers, and DevOps professionals aiming to build scalable, cost-effective, and secure applications in the cloud.

With the right storage strategies, you can ensure optimal performance, redundancy, and compliance—ensuring your data is always available, protected, and aligned with your organization's needs.

Networking: Virtual Networks, Load Balancers, and Gateways

Azure networking services form the digital backbone of your cloud infrastructure. A robust networking setup ensures seamless communication between services, high availability, and secure access—both within Azure and from on-premises environments. Whether you're running a small web app or a global enterprise system, understanding Azure's networking components is crucial for performance, scalability, and security.

This section covers three critical components:

- **Virtual Networks (VNets)**

- **Load Balancers**

- **Virtual Network Gateways**

Virtual Networks (VNets)

A **Virtual Network (VNet)** is the core building block of an Azure private network. It enables many types of Azure resources to securely communicate with each other, the internet, and on-premises networks.

Key Characteristics

- **Isolation**: VNets are isolated from each other, like VLANs.

- **Subnets**: VNets can be divided into subnets to segment workloads.

- **IP Addressing**: Use custom private IP address ranges (IPv4 and IPv6).

- **Connectivity**: Connect VNets to on-premises networks using VPNs or ExpressRoute.

Creating a VNet

```
az network vnet create \
  --name MyVNet \
  --resource-group MyResourceGroup \
  --address-prefix 10.0.0.0/16 \
  --subnet-name MySubnet \
  --subnet-prefix 10.0.1.0/24
```

This command creates a VNet with one subnet in the specified address space.

Use Cases

- Hosting applications and services securely

- Segmenting network traffic using subnets

- Routing and controlling inbound/outbound access

- Establishing hybrid connectivity

Subnets and Network Security Groups (NSGs)

Subnets allow logical separation of services within a VNet. Each subnet can have its own Network Security Group (NSG), which acts like a firewall for traffic filtering.

NSG Example

```
az network nsg create \
  --resource-group MyResourceGroup \
  --name MyNSG

az network nsg rule create \
  --resource-group MyResourceGroup \
  --nsg-name MyNSG \
  --name AllowHTTP \
  --protocol Tcp \
  --direction Inbound \
  --source-address-prefixes '*' \
  --source-port-ranges '*' \
  --destination-address-prefixes '*' \
  --destination-port-ranges 80 \
  --access Allow \
  --priority 100
```

Attach the NSG to a subnet or NIC:

```
az network vnet subnet update \
  --vnet-name MyVNet \
  --name MySubnet \
  --resource-group MyResourceGroup \
  --network-security-group MyNSG
```

Azure DNS and Custom DNS

Azure provides internal name resolution for resources within the same VNet. However, for custom domain resolution or integration with enterprise systems, you can assign custom DNS servers.

```
az network vnet update \
  --name MyVNet \
  --resource-group MyResourceGroup \
  --dns-servers 10.1.1.4 10.1.2.5
```

VNet Peering

VNet Peering enables low-latency, high-bandwidth connectivity between two VNets in the same or different regions.

```
az network vnet peering create \
  --name Peer1To2 \
  --resource-group MyResourceGroup \
  --vnet-name VNet1 \
  --remote-vnet VNet2 \
  --allow-vnet-access
```

Use Cases:

- Microservice architecture with resource segregation

- Interconnecting development, staging, and production networks

---

Azure Load Balancer

Azure Load Balancer distributes inbound traffic to healthy VM instances. It operates at Layer 4 (TCP/UDP) and is ideal for high-performance, low-latency applications.

Types

1. **Public Load Balancer** – Exposes services to the internet.

2. **Internal Load Balancer** – Distributes traffic within a VNet.

Key Concepts

- **Backend Pools**: List of VM instances to distribute traffic to.

- **Health Probes**: Monitors the status of backend instances.

- **Load Balancing Rules**: Define how traffic is distributed.

Creating a Basic Public Load Balancer

```
az network public-ip create \
  --name MyPublicIP \
  --resource-group MyResourceGroup \
  --allocation-method Static
```

```
az network lb create \
  --name MyLoadBalancer \
  --resource-group MyResourceGroup \
  --frontend-ip-name MyFrontEnd \
  --backend-pool-name MyBackEndPool \
  --public-ip-address MyPublicIP
```

Add a rule:

```
az network lb rule create \
  --resource-group MyResourceGroup \
  --lb-name MyLoadBalancer \
  --name MyHTTPRule \
  --protocol tcp \
  --frontend-port 80 \
  --backend-port 80 \
  --frontend-ip-name MyFrontEnd \
  --backend-pool-name MyBackEndPool \
  --probe-name MyHealthProbe
```

Create a health probe:

```
az network lb probe create \
  --resource-group MyResourceGroup \
  --lb-name MyLoadBalancer \
  --name MyHealthProbe \
  --protocol tcp \
  --port 80
```

Azure Application Gateway

While Load Balancer operates at Layer 4, **Application Gateway** works at Layer 7, enabling advanced routing based on URLs, host headers, and SSL termination.

Features:

- Path-based routing

- SSL offloading

- Web Application Firewall (WAF) integration

```
az network application-gateway create \
  --name MyAppGateway \
  --location eastus \
  --resource-group MyResourceGroup \
  --capacity 2 \
  --sku WAF_Medium \
  --vnet-name MyVNet \
  --subnet MySubnet
```

Use Application Gateway for modern web apps that require TLS termination and intelligent routing.

Azure Virtual Network Gateway

Virtual Network Gateway is the endpoint for **VPN** or **ExpressRoute** connections, enabling secure communication between Azure VNets and on-premises networks.

VPN Gateway Types

- **Route-based** (dynamic routing): Preferred and more flexible

- **Policy-based** (static routing): Legacy support

Site-to-Site VPN Setup

1. **Create Gateway Subnet**

```
az network vnet subnet create \
  --name GatewaySubnet \
  --resource-group MyResourceGroup \
  --vnet-name MyVNet \
  --address-prefix 10.0.255.0/27
```

2. **Create Public IP for Gateway**

```
az network public-ip create \
  --resource-group MyResourceGroup \
```

```
--name MyGatewayIP \
--allocation-method Dynamic
```

3. **Create Virtual Network Gateway**

```
az network vnet-gateway create \
  --name MyVNetGateway \
  --resource-group MyResourceGroup \
  --public-ip-address MyGatewayIP \
  --vnet MyVNet \
  --gateway-type Vpn \
  --vpn-type RouteBased \
  --sku VpnGw1 \
  --no-wait
```

4. **Connect to On-Prem VPN Device**

You define a **Local Network Gateway** (on-prem network) and then create a connection between the VNet Gateway and the Local Gateway.

ExpressRoute

For enterprises needing private, high-throughput connections, Azure **ExpressRoute** bypasses the public internet. It connects your on-prem network to Azure via a dedicated fiber circuit.

Benefits:

- Private connectivity

- Higher bandwidth (up to 100 Gbps)

- Consistent latency and reliability

Use Cases:

- Large data transfers

- Hybrid cloud architectures

- Regulatory requirements

Network Watcher and Monitoring

Azure offers **Network Watcher** to monitor, diagnose, and gain insights into your network.

Features

- **Topology Viewer**

- **Connection Troubleshooting**

- **Packet Captures**

- **NSG Flow Logs**

```
az network watcher configure \
  --resource-group MyResourceGroup \
  --locations eastus \
  --enabled true
```

Enable NSG flow logs:

```
az network watcher flow-log configure \
  --resource-group MyResourceGroup \
  --nsg MyNSG \
  --enabled true \
  --retention 7 \
  --storage-account mystorageaccount
```

Best Practices

- **Use NSGs at both subnet and NIC level** for granular control.

- **Segment workloads** using subnets, peering, and Application Security Groups (ASGs).

- **Apply diagnostics** and enable logging for all networking components.

- **Enforce Private Endpoints** for services like Azure Storage and SQL to prevent public access.

- **Use Application Gateway** for web-facing workloads needing WAF and TLS offload.

- **Implement redundancy** with Load Balancer and Availability Zones.

Conclusion

Azure networking services offer the flexibility and power to design secure, scalable, and highly available infrastructure. By mastering Virtual Networks, Load Balancers, and Gateways, you can build systems that handle modern traffic patterns, resist threats, and scale globally. As your application architecture grows, these components will help ensure your infrastructure evolves smoothly while staying secure and performant.

Databases: Azure SQL, Cosmos DB, and More

Data is at the heart of nearly every application. Whether it's a simple web app storing user profiles or a global e-commerce platform handling real-time transactions and analytics, databases are essential. Azure offers a robust portfolio of database services catering to various use cases—from relational systems like Azure SQL Database to globally distributed NoSQL databases like Cosmos DB, and even open-source engines like MySQL, PostgreSQL, and MariaDB.

This section provides an in-depth exploration of Azure's core database offerings:

- **Azure SQL Database**

- **Azure Cosmos DB**

- **Azure Database for MySQL, PostgreSQL, and MariaDB**

- **Database migration and integration tools**

- **Security, scaling, and best practices**

Azure SQL Database

Azure SQL Database is a fully managed platform-as-a-service (PaaS) database engine built on Microsoft SQL Server. It eliminates the need for managing physical hardware, patching, backups, and high availability configurations.

Key Features

- Intelligent performance tuning and query optimization

- Built-in high availability with 99.99% uptime SLA

- Automatic backups and geo-redundancy

- Threat detection and vulnerability assessments

- Supports both single and elastic pool models

Deployment Options

1. **Single Database** – Isolated database with dedicated resources

2. **Elastic Pool** – Shared resources for multiple databases

3. **Managed Instance** – Full SQL Server compatibility in PaaS

Creating an Azure SQL Database (CLI)

```
# Create a logical SQL server
az sql server create \
  --name my-sql-server \
  --resource-group myResourceGroup \
  --location eastus \
  --admin-user myadmin \
  --admin-password P@ssw0rd123

# Create the database
az sql db create \
  --resource-group myResourceGroup \
  --server my-sql-server \
  --name mydatabase \
  --service-objective S1
```

Firewall and Connection

Allow Azure services and your IP to access the database:

```
az sql server firewall-rule create \
  --resource-group myResourceGroup \
  --server my-sql-server \
```

```
--name AllowMyIP \
--start-ip-address <YOUR_IP> \
--end-ip-address <YOUR_IP>
```

Connect using tools like SQL Server Management Studio (SSMS), Azure Data Studio, or programming libraries (ADO.NET, JDBC, etc.).

Performance Tiers

- **Basic, Standard, Premium** (DTUs)

- **General Purpose, Business Critical, Hyperscale** (vCore)

Choose based on budget, performance, and scaling requirements.

Azure Cosmos DB

Azure Cosmos DB is a globally distributed, multi-model NoSQL database service. It supports key-value, document, graph, and column-family data models with APIs for MongoDB, Cassandra, Gremlin, SQL (Core), and Table.

Key Features

- Multi-region replication with automatic failover

- Millisecond response times, guaranteed SLA

- Multiple consistency models (strong, bounded staleness, session, eventual)

- Globally distributed data for real-time access

- Elastic scaling of throughput and storage

Creating a Cosmos DB Account (CLI)

```
az cosmosdb create \
  --name mycosmosdb \
  --resource-group myResourceGroup \
  --locations regionName=eastus failoverPriority=0
isZoneRedundant=False \
  --default-consistency-level Session
```

Create a database and container:

```
az cosmosdb sql database create \
  --account-name mycosmosdb \
  --name mydb \
  --resource-group myResourceGroup

az cosmosdb sql container create \
  --account-name mycosmosdb \
  --database-name mydb \
  --name mycontainer \
  --partition-key-path "/userid"
```

Use Cases

- IoT and telemetry data

- Real-time personalization and recommendations

- Multi-region applications with low latency needs

- Shopping cart and user session management

Azure Database for MySQL, PostgreSQL, and MariaDB

Azure offers managed versions of popular open-source relational databases, with full community edition support.

Shared Features

- Automated backups, patching, and monitoring

- Built-in high availability (zone redundant)

- Flexible scaling of compute and storage

- Security through VNet integration and firewall rules

Azure Database for MySQL

Use Azure Database for MySQL for LAMP stack apps, WordPress, and eCommerce platforms like Magento.

Creating MySQL Server:

```
az mysql server create \
  --resource-group myResourceGroup \
  --name mymysqlserver \
  --location eastus \
  --admin-user myadmin \
  --admin-password MyPassword123! \
  --sku-name B_Gen5_1
```

Azure Database for PostgreSQL

Ideal for GIS, analytics, Django apps, and machine learning pipelines.

Azure offers two options:

- **Single Server (legacy)**

- **Flexible Server (recommended)** – Greater control, custom maintenance windows, stop/start capabilities

Creating a PostgreSQL Flexible Server:

```
az postgres flexible-server create \
  --resource-group myResourceGroup \
  --name mypgserver \
  --location eastus \
  --admin-user pgadmin \
  --admin-password StrongP@ss123 \
  --sku-name Standard_D2s_v3 \
  --tier GeneralPurpose
```

Azure Database for MariaDB

Compatible with MySQL, this is useful for apps like Moodle and Joomla. Similar CLI commands apply.

Data Migration with Azure Database Migration Service

Azure Database Migration Service (DMS) helps migrate on-prem databases to Azure with minimal downtime. It supports migrations from:

- SQL Server to Azure SQL
- MySQL/PostgreSQL to Azure Database for MySQL/PostgreSQL
- MongoDB to Cosmos DB

You can perform **online** or **offline** migrations.

Steps:

1. Create a DMS instance.
2. Create a migration project and choose source/target.
3. Run assessment and start migration.

Scaling and Performance Optimization

Horizontal vs Vertical Scaling

- **Vertical scaling**: Increase compute resources (vCores/DTUs).
- **Horizontal scaling**: Shard data or add replicas (Cosmos DB).

Indexing

- SQL Server: Clustered, non-clustered, columnstore indexes
- Cosmos DB: Automatic indexing with custom policy options

Query Optimization

- Analyze query plans in SQL Server
- Use **Query Performance Insight** for slow queries
- Cosmos DB offers **Query Metrics API**

Backup, High Availability, and Disaster Recovery

Azure SQL Database

- **Automatic Backups** retained up to 35 days (configurable)

- **Geo-replication** for business continuity

- **Failover groups** for multi-region HA

Cosmos DB

- **Multi-region writes**

- **Automatic failover**

- **Point-in-time restore**

PostgreSQL Flexible Server

- **Geo-redundant backup**

- **High Availability Zones**

Security

- **Encryption**: Data at rest and in transit (TLS 1.2+)

- **Access Control**: Firewall rules, VNet integration, Azure AD authentication

- **Auditing and Threat Detection**: Built-in alerts and logs for suspicious activity

```
az sql db audit-policy update \
  --name mydatabase \
  --resource-group myResourceGroup \
  --server my-sql-server \
  --state Enabled \
  --storage-account myauditstorage
```

Monitoring and Automation

Use **Azure Monitor** and **Log Analytics** for:

- Query performance

- Deadlocks

- CPU/memory usage

- Storage trends

Enable alerts and autoscaling where possible:

```
az monitor metrics alert create \
  --resource-group myResourceGroup \
  --name HighDTUUsage \
  --scopes
/subscriptions/.../resourceGroups/.../providers/Microsoft.Sql/server
s/my-sql-server/databases/mydatabase \
  --condition "avg dtu_consumption_percent > 80" \
  --description "Alert for high DTU usage"
```

Best Practices

- Use **managed identities** for app authentication to databases

- Keep **firewalls tight**, allow only necessary IP ranges

- Set up **automatic tuning** for SQL Database

- Schedule **regular assessments** with Azure SQL Advisor

- For Cosmos DB, **choose partition keys carefully** to avoid hot partitions

Conclusion

Azure provides a comprehensive set of database services that suit nearly every application architecture—from traditional transactional systems to cutting-edge real-time analytics and globally distributed apps. With managed services for SQL, NoSQL, and open-source engines, developers can focus on building applications while Azure handles maintenance, scaling, and security. Understanding the right service for your use case, paired with proper configuration and monitoring, ensures long-term success and optimal performance in the cloud.

Identity: Azure Active Directory Basics

Managing identity and access is central to ensuring security and operational efficiency in cloud environments. Azure Active Directory (Azure AD) is Microsoft's cloud-based identity and access management service. It allows organizations to manage user identities, authenticate users and applications, and enforce access policies for Azure resources and other integrated services.

Azure AD underpins almost all services in Azure, making it vital for anyone working in cloud computing to understand its concepts, capabilities, and configurations.

This section explores:

- Core concepts of Azure AD

- User and group management

- Role-Based Access Control (RBAC)

- Application registration and authentication

- Conditional Access and security features

- Integration with on-premises AD and other identity providers

What is Azure Active Directory?

Azure Active Directory is a multi-tenant, cloud-based directory and identity management service that combines core directory services, application access management, and identity protection.

It serves the following purposes:

- **Authentication**: Who are you?

- **Authorization**: What are you allowed to do?

- **Single Sign-On (SSO)**: Seamless access to multiple resources

- **Device Management**: Conditional access based on device status

- **Access Governance**: Policies and auditing for secure access

Azure AD supports **OAuth2.0**, **OpenID Connect**, **SAML**, **WS-Federation**, and **LDAP** (via Azure AD Domain Services).

Users and Groups

Creating Users

Users can be created manually or synced from on-prem Active Directory using **Azure AD Connect**.

```
az ad user create \
  --display-name "Jane Doe" \
  --user-principal-name janedoe@yourtenant.onmicrosoft.com \
  --password "P@ssword123!" \
  --force-change-password-next-login true
```

Alternatively, manage users via the Azure Portal under **Azure Active Directory > Users**.

Groups

Groups simplify permission management. Users are added to groups, and those groups are granted access to resources.

There are two types:

- **Security Groups**: Used to manage access to Azure resources

- **Microsoft 365 Groups**: Used in collaboration scenarios (e.g., Microsoft Teams, SharePoint)

```
az ad group create \
  --display-name "DevTeam" \
  --mail-nickname "devteam"
```

Add a user to a group:

```
az ad group member add \
  --group "DevTeam" \
  --member-id <UserObjectId>
```

Role-Based Access Control (RBAC)

RBAC in Azure allows you to assign permissions to users, groups, and applications at different scopes: **subscription**, **resource group**, or **resource** level.

Key Roles

- **Owner**: Full access including role assignment

- **Contributor**: Full access except role assignment

- **Reader**: View only access

- **Custom Roles**: Defined with JSON permissions

Assigning a Role (CLI)

```
az role assignment create \
  --assignee <UserObjectId or Email> \
  --role "Contributor" \
  --scope
/subscriptions/<subscriptionId>/resourceGroups/<resourceGroupName>
```

You can view role assignments:

```
az role assignment list --all
```

RBAC is preferable over classic access control because of its granularity and auditing capabilities.

Application Registration

When developing apps that integrate with Azure or Microsoft 365, you register them in Azure AD to enable authentication and permissions management.

Why Register an App?

- Obtain client IDs and secrets

- Define redirect URIs

- Enable API permissions (Microsoft Graph, custom APIs)

Registering an Application (Portal)

1. Go to **Azure Active Directory > App registrations**

2. Click **New registration**

3. Provide a name and redirect URI

4. Register and note the **Application (client) ID** and **Directory (tenant) ID**

Using Azure CLI

```
az ad app create \
  --display-name "MyWebApp" \
  --identifier-uris "https://mywebapp.contoso.com" \
  --reply-urls "https://mywebapp.contoso.com/auth" \
  --password "SuperSecret123!"
```

Create a service principal:

```
az ad sp create --id <appId>
```

Authentication and Authorization Flows

Azure AD supports multiple flows depending on the app type:

- **Authorization Code Flow**: Used for web and native apps

- **Client Credentials Flow**: Used for daemon apps/services

- **Device Code Flow**: Used for CLI or device-based access

- **On-Behalf-Of Flow**: Web APIs calling other APIs

Use libraries like **MSAL (Microsoft Authentication Library)** or **ADAL (deprecated)** for integrating Azure AD with applications.

Example with MSAL.js:

```
const msalConfig = {
  auth: {
```

```
    clientId: "your-client-id",
    authority: "https://login.microsoftonline.com/your-tenant-id",
    redirectUri: "https://yourapp.com/auth"
  }
};

const msalInstance = new msal.PublicClientApplication(msalConfig);

msalInstance.loginPopup().then(response => {
  console.log("Access Token:", response.accessToken);
});
```

Conditional Access

Conditional Access provides adaptive access control by evaluating signals like user, location, device, and risk level.

Policies You Can Define:

- Block access from risky IPs

- Require MFA for external users

- Enforce access only from compliant devices

Set up Conditional Access via **Azure AD > Security > Conditional Access**.

Example conditions:

- Users in "All Guests"

- Accessing "All cloud apps"

- Require MFA and compliant device

Multi-Factor Authentication (MFA)

Azure MFA strengthens identity protection by requiring at least two of the following:

- Something you know (password)

- Something you have (phone, hardware token)

- Something you are (biometrics)

Enable MFA via **Azure AD > Security > MFA**. You can enforce MFA using Conditional Access or per-user MFA settings.

Azure AD Connect

Azure AD Connect synchronizes on-prem Active Directory with Azure AD, enabling hybrid identity scenarios.

Features:

- Password hash synchronization

- Federation using AD FS

- Seamless Single Sign-On (SSO)

Download the Azure AD Connect tool and configure it to match your sync requirements. Customize OU filtering, user attribute selection, and synchronization schedule.

Azure AD Domain Services

Azure AD DS provides managed domain services like LDAP, Kerberos, and domain join—without deploying Domain Controllers.

Use it when:

- You have legacy apps requiring AD features

- You want secure domain-joined VMs in Azure

- You need group policy support

Monitoring and Auditing

Azure AD logs are critical for security and compliance.

Access logs via **Azure AD > Sign-ins** and **Audit logs**, or integrate with **Azure Monitor** or **Log Analytics**.

Track events such as:

- User sign-ins and failures

- Role assignments

- Application consent grants

- Conditional Access policy evaluations

Example: Create an alert for repeated login failures.

```
az monitor log-analytics query \
  --workspace <workspaceId> \
  --analytics-query "SigninLogs | where ResultType != 0 | summarize
count() by UserPrincipalName"
```

Security Recommendations

- **Enforce MFA** for all users

- **Use Conditional Access** to minimize attack surface

- **Avoid legacy authentication protocols**

- **Use managed identities** instead of storing secrets in code

- **Regularly review role assignments**

- **Enable Identity Protection** for risk-based controls

Best Practices

- Use **least privilege** when assigning roles

- Avoid using **Owner** role unless absolutely necessary

- **Use groups** to assign roles, not individuals

- Rotate app secrets regularly

- **Enable Self-Service Password Reset** for users

- Use **Privileged Identity Management (PIM)** for Just-in-Time (JIT) admin access

---

Conclusion

Azure Active Directory is a foundational component of every Azure environment, providing identity and access management across the cloud ecosystem. By understanding users, roles, application registration, and Conditional Access, you can architect secure, scalable solutions. Integrating with Azure AD also simplifies authentication and enables advanced security features, reducing risks while improving user experience. Mastery of Azure AD is essential for every Azure administrator, developer, and architect seeking to implement modern, secure cloud solutions.

Chapter 4: Building Your First Azure Project

Planning Your Project: Goals and Requirements

Embarking on your first Azure project is a pivotal step in your cloud journey. Whether you're creating a personal portfolio site, a backend for a mobile app, or deploying enterprise-level services, careful planning is essential to ensure success. Planning involves defining project goals, understanding requirements, selecting the right Azure services, estimating costs, designing architecture, and setting up security and governance measures. This foundational phase can drastically improve your deployment efficiency, cost-effectiveness, and scalability.

Defining Project Goals

Before writing any code or spinning up resources in Azure, take time to clearly define the **goals of your project**. Goals help you focus on the **purpose** and determine the **technical scope**.

Sample Project Goal Statements:

- Deploy a scalable and secure web application for tracking user tasks

- Host a portfolio website with CI/CD and global availability

- Implement a backend API for a mobile application with authentication

- Migrate an on-premise database to Azure with minimal downtime

Ask yourself:

- Who are the users?

- What problems are you solving?

- What will success look like?

- What are the short-term and long-term goals?

Clearly stated objectives will guide your architecture, technology choices, and milestones.

Gathering and Analyzing Requirements

After defining your goals, identify the **functional** and **non-functional requirements**:

Functional Requirements:

- User authentication

- CRUD operations for tasks or data

- API endpoints for mobile apps

- Integration with third-party services (e.g., payment gateways)

Non-Functional Requirements:

- Scalability (handle thousands of users)

- Availability (99.9% uptime)

- Security (data encryption, RBAC)

- Compliance (GDPR, HIPAA)

- Performance (response times under 200ms)

You should also define **business constraints**, such as:

- Budget limits

- Deadlines

- Skillset of the development team

- Regulatory or legal considerations

Create a requirements document to formalize these inputs, which you'll reference throughout development and deployment.

Choosing the Right Azure Services

Azure offers a wide range of services—choose the ones best aligned to your project's needs.

Example: Web Application with Database

Requirement	Azure Service
Hosting the frontend	Azure App Service or Static Web Apps
User authentication	Azure Active Directory B2C
Persistent data storage	Azure SQL Database or Cosmos DB
Serverless business logic	Azure Functions
Messaging system	Azure Service Bus or Event Grid
Monitoring & logging	Azure Monitor, App Insights

Avoid overengineering—start simple and build incrementally.

Designing Your Architecture

At this point, begin sketching your cloud architecture. Consider:

1. **Resource Group Layout**

2. **Networking Requirements** (e.g., Virtual Network, Private Endpoints)

3. **Data Flow and Integration Points**

4. **Service Interactions**

5. **Scaling Strategy**

Use the **Azure Architecture Center** for proven patterns. Tools like **Azure Diagrams, Draw.io**, or **Visio** help visualize architecture.

Example Logical Architecture:

- Azure Front Door for global load balancing

- App Service for hosting the frontend

- API Management + Azure Functions for backend logic

- Azure SQL Database for data persistence

- Azure Key Vault for secrets management

- Application Insights for telemetry

Plan for scalability by identifying services that support auto-scaling and designing stateless services where possible.

Budgeting and Cost Estimation

Use the **Azure Pricing Calculator** to estimate the monthly cost of your architecture.

1. Go to https://azure.com/pricing

2. Select services like App Service, SQL Database, Storage, etc.

3. Enter expected usage levels (compute hours, data size, IOPS)

4. Review monthly costs and adjust SKUs or regions as needed

Also, enable **Azure Cost Management + Billing** in your subscription to:

- Track actual vs projected costs

- Set **budgets and alerts**

- Analyze usage trends over time

Set cost boundaries in your planning document. Use **Azure Reservations** or **Savings Plans** for predictable workloads.

Security Planning

Security should be built into the design from the start.

Considerations:

- **Identity and Access Control**: Use RBAC and avoid broad permissions.

- **Data Security**: Use encryption at rest and in transit.

- **Network Security**: Secure services with Private Endpoints, NSGs, and Firewalls.

- **Secrets Management**: Store credentials and secrets in Azure Key Vault.

- **Authentication and Authorization**: Use Azure AD or B2C for identity management.

Example CLI to create a Key Vault:

```
az keyvault create --name MyKeyVault --resource-group
MyResourceGroup --location eastus
```

Store a secret:

```
az keyvault secret set --vault-name MyKeyVault --name "DbPassword" -
-value "SuperSecret123!"
```

Planning for High Availability and Disaster Recovery

Your project should be designed for **resilience** from the start.

Strategies:

- Deploy across **multiple Availability Zones**

- Use **Azure Traffic Manager** or **Front Door** for global load balancing

- Enable **Geo-Replication** for databases

- Take regular **backups** and test restores

For mission-critical applications, design with **Active-Active** deployments where possible.

DevOps and CI/CD Readiness

Plan how code will be built, tested, and deployed.

Azure supports many DevOps tools:

- **GitHub Actions**

- **Azure DevOps Pipelines**

- **Bitbucket Pipelines**

- **Jenkins**

Consider creating pipelines for:

- Continuous Integration (build + unit tests)

- Continuous Deployment (automatic deploy to staging or production)

- Infrastructure as Code (using Bicep, ARM, or Terraform)

Example: Basic GitHub Actions workflow for App Service

```
name: Deploy to Azure

on:
  push:
    branches:
      - main

jobs:
  build-and-deploy:
    runs-on: ubuntu-latest
    steps:
      - uses: actions/checkout@v2
      - uses: azure/webapps-deploy@v2
        with:
          app-name: 'myappservice'
          publish-profile: ${{ secrets.AZURE_WEBAPP_PUBLISH_PROFILE }}
          package: '.'
```

Documentation and Collaboration

Plan how you'll maintain and share project knowledge. This includes:

- Project architecture diagrams

- API documentation (e.g., Swagger/OpenAPI)

- Setup scripts and environment variables

- Onboarding guides for new team members

Use tools like:

- **Azure DevOps Wiki**

- **Confluence**

- **Notion**

- **Markdown in GitHub repositories**

Version-control all documentation to track changes over time.

Establishing Governance

To prevent chaos as your project scales, implement basic governance controls:

- **Naming Conventions**: Standardize naming across all resources

- **Tagging Strategy**: Tag by environment, owner, cost center

- **Policies**: Use **Azure Policy** to enforce rules (e.g., block unsupported regions)

- **Blueprints**: Predefine compliant environments

Example Azure Policy to block non-EU regions:

```
{
  "if": {
    "field": "location",
    "notIn": ["northeurope", "westeurope"]
  },
  "then": {
    "effect": "deny"
  }
}
```

Timeline and Milestones

Plan your development in phases with clear milestones.

Example Project Timeline:

Phase	Duration	Key Deliverables
Planning & Setup	1 week	Requirements, architecture, cost estimation
Initial Development	2 weeks	Core features, database integration
Testing & Hardening	1 week	Load testing, security reviews
Deployment & Review	1 week	Launch, monitoring, feedback collection

Use tools like **Azure Boards**, **Jira**, or **Trello** to manage sprints and backlog.

Conclusion

Planning your first Azure project is about more than just picking services—it's a comprehensive process of defining objectives, analyzing requirements, designing architecture, budgeting effectively, and laying down solid foundations for security and governance. Taking the time to plan well will save you significant time and effort during implementation, reduce costs, and increase the likelihood of long-term success. In the next section, we'll move from planning into hands-on deployment, starting with launching your first web app on Azure.

Deploying a Web App on Azure

Deploying a web application on Azure is a streamlined and scalable process that enables developers to publish applications to the cloud with minimal infrastructure management. Azure offers various hosting services for web applications, but the most commonly used and developer-friendly option is **Azure App Service**—a fully managed Platform as a Service (PaaS) that allows you to deploy web applications, RESTful APIs, and mobile backends in your preferred language and framework.

This section walks through deploying a web app from planning and setup, to deployment, scaling, and monitoring using Azure App Service, CLI tools, and optionally GitHub Actions.

Overview of Azure App Service

Azure App Service provides:

- Managed infrastructure (automatic patching, scaling, high availability)

- Language support (.NET, Java, Node.js, Python, PHP, Ruby)

- Deployment options (Git, ZIP, Docker, GitHub Actions, Azure DevOps)

- Built-in load balancing and auto-scaling

- Integration with Azure Monitor and Application Insights

App Service runs on **App Service Plans**, which define compute resources and pricing tiers. It supports both Windows and Linux environments.

Setting Up Your Environment

Before deploying your app, ensure you have:

- An Azure subscription

- Azure CLI installed and authenticated (`az login`)

- Your application code (e.g., Node.js, Flask, ASP.NET Core)

- GitHub account if you plan to use GitHub Actions for CI/CD

Let's start by setting up the core infrastructure.

Step 1: Create a Resource Group

A resource group is a container for related Azure resources.

```
az group create --name WebAppRG --location eastus
```

Step 2: Create an App Service Plan

The App Service Plan defines the region, scaling, and pricing tier.

```
az appservice plan create \
  --name WebAppPlan \
  --resource-group WebAppRG \
  --sku B1 \
  --is-linux
```

This command creates a **Basic (B1)** Linux-based plan, which is suitable for development and testing.

Step 3: Create the Web App

```
az webapp create \
  --resource-group WebAppRG \
  --plan WebAppPlan \
  --name myuniquename123 \
  --runtime "NODE|18-lts" \
  --deployment-local-git
```

You'll receive a Git URL like:

```
https://myuniquename123.scm.azurewebsites.net/myuniquename123.git
```

Push your code using Git:

```
git remote add azure https://<your-app>.scm.azurewebsites.net/<your-app>.git
git push azure main
```

Replace <your-app> with the actual name returned from the CLI.

Step 4: Deploy via ZIP Upload (Alternative)

If you don't want to use Git, you can zip your application folder and deploy it:

```
az webapp deployment source config-zip \
  --resource-group WebAppRG \
  --name myuniquename123 \
  --src path/to/app.zip
```

Step 5: Configure Application Settings

You can define app settings and environment variables:

```
az webapp config appsettings set \
  --resource-group WebAppRG \
  --name myuniquename123 \
  --settings "ENV=production" "API_KEY=abc123"
```

To view current settings:

```
az webapp config appsettings list \
  --resource-group WebAppRG \
  --name myuniquename123
```

Step 6: Enable Logging

Enable diagnostic logs to help debug deployment or runtime issues:

```
az webapp log config \
  --name myuniquename123 \
  --resource-group WebAppRG \
  --application-logging filesystem \
  --level information
```

View logs via streaming:

```
az webapp log tail \
  --name myuniquename123 \
  --resource-group WebAppRG
```

Step 7: Enable Custom Domain and HTTPS

If you have a custom domain, you can map it to your web app:

```
az webapp config hostname add \
  --webapp-name myuniquename123 \
  --resource-group WebAppRG \
```

```
--hostname www.mycustomdomain.com
```

You'll need to verify domain ownership via DNS records, then you can enable HTTPS:

```
az webapp config ssl bind \
  --certificate-thumbprint <thumbprint> \
  --ssl-type SNI \
  --resource-group WebAppRG \
  --name myuniquename123
```

Certificates can be managed manually or via **App Service Managed Certificates**.

Step 8: Scaling and Performance Tuning

You can scale App Service vertically or horizontally.

Scale Vertically (Upgrade Plan)

```
az appservice plan update \
  --name WebAppPlan \
  --resource-group WebAppRG \
  --sku S1
```

Scale Horizontally (Add Instances)

```
az appservice plan update \
  --name WebAppPlan \
  --resource-group WebAppRG \
  --number-of-workers 3
```

Enable Autoscaling

Define autoscale rules based on CPU, memory, or time of day using Azure Monitor.

```
az monitor autoscale create \
  --resource-group WebAppRG \
  --resource WebAppPlan \
  --resource-type Microsoft.Web/serverfarms \
  --name autoscale-rule \
  --min-count 1 \
  --max-count 5 \
  --count 2
```

Step 9: CI/CD with GitHub Actions

Integrate GitHub with App Service for continuous deployment.

```
az webapp deployment github-actions add \
  --repo <GitHubRepoURL> \
  --branch main \
  --name myuniquename123 \
  --resource-group WebAppRG \
  --login-with-github
```

This creates a GitHub Actions workflow in your repo, automating build and deployment.

Example Workflow Snippet:

```
jobs:
  build-and-deploy:
    runs-on: ubuntu-latest
    steps:
    - name: Checkout code
      uses: actions/checkout@v2
    - name: Setup Node
      uses: actions/setup-node@v2
      with:
        node-version: '18'
    - run: npm install
    - run: npm run build
    - uses: azure/webapps-deploy@v2
      with:
        app-name: 'myuniquename123'
        publish-profile: ${{ secrets.AZURE_WEBAPP_PUBLISH_PROFILE }}
        package: '.'
```

Step 10: Monitor and Maintain

Use **Azure Monitor** and **Application Insights** to gain insights into application health, performance, and usage patterns.

Enable Application Insights:

```
az monitor app-insights component create \
  --app MyAppInsights \
  --location eastus \
  --resource-group WebAppRG \
  --application-type web
```

Link it to your App Service:

```
az webapp config appsettings set \
  --resource-group WebAppRG \
  --name myuniquename123 \
  --settings APPINSIGHTS_INSTRUMENTATIONKEY=<your-instrumentation-key>
```

Use Application Insights to monitor:

- Request rates and response times

- Failures and exceptions

- Custom telemetry

- Availability tests

Cleanup Resources (Optional)

If you want to delete all resources related to your app:

```
az group delete --name WebAppRG --yes --no-wait
```

Best Practices

- Use **deployment slots** for staging environments before going live.

- Enable **auto-heal rules** to restart instances on specific conditions.

- Regularly rotate credentials and secrets.

- Use **managed identities** for app-to-service authentication.

- Apply **resource tagging** for cost management and ownership.

Conclusion

Deploying a web app on Azure using App Service is a powerful way to bring your ideas to life with minimal infrastructure overhead. With support for multiple languages, seamless CI/CD integration, robust scaling options, and rich observability tools, Azure App Service provides everything you need to deploy, run, and grow your application. Once deployed, your focus can shift from managing infrastructure to delivering great user experiences and iterating on features rapidly. In the next section, we'll explore how to connect your web app to a database to store and retrieve dynamic data.

Setting Up a Simple Database

In most applications, a web frontend is only half of the story—the other half lives in the backend where data is stored, retrieved, and modified. Whether you're building a task management tool, an eCommerce platform, or a blogging system, you'll need a robust, scalable database to persist data reliably. Azure provides a rich ecosystem of managed databases that can easily be integrated with your applications.

This section guides you through the process of setting up a simple database using **Azure SQL Database**, connecting it to your web app, and managing it through tools, code, and security best practices. We'll also briefly touch on alternatives such as **Cosmos DB** and **Azure Database for MySQL**.

Choosing the Right Database Service

The first step is choosing the right type of database for your application. For this example, we'll use **Azure SQL Database**, which is ideal for structured data and supports the familiar SQL Server engine. This service is fully managed and provides built-in backups, scaling, and high availability.

Use Azure SQL Database when:

- Your application uses structured, relational data

- You want full SQL support (joins, stored procedures, triggers)

- You're migrating from an on-prem SQL Server

Other options:

- **Azure Cosmos DB** – For NoSQL and globally distributed apps

- **Azure Database for MySQL/PostgreSQL** – For open-source relational systems

- **Azure Table Storage** – For key-value stores or lightweight data needs

Step 1: Create a SQL Server and Database

Let's start by creating the infrastructure to host our database.

```
az group create --name DBResourceGroup --location eastus
```

Create the logical SQL server:

```
az sql server create \
  --name mywebappsqlserver \
  --resource-group DBResourceGroup \
  --location eastus \
  --admin-user dbadmin \
  --admin-password P@ssword123!
```

Create the database:

```
az sql db create \
  --resource-group DBResourceGroup \
  --server mywebappsqlserver \
  --name mywebappdb \
  --service-objective S0
```

This creates a basic SQL database with the S0 service tier, suitable for development or small workloads.

Step 2: Configure Access

To allow external access to your database (e.g., from your local machine or App Service), configure firewall rules.

Allow your IP:

```
az sql server firewall-rule create \
```

```
--resource-group DBResourceGroup \
--server mywebappsqlserver \
--name AllowMyIP \
--start-ip-address <YOUR_IP> \
--end-ip-address <YOUR_IP>
```

To allow Azure services (like App Service) to access the database:

```
az sql server firewall-rule create \
  --resource-group DBResourceGroup \
  --server mywebappsqlserver \
  --name AllowAzureServices \
  --start-ip-address 0.0.0.0 \
  --end-ip-address 0.0.0.0
```

Step 3: Connect Using SQL Tools

You can connect to your Azure SQL Database using tools like:

- **Azure Data Studio**

- **SQL Server Management Studio (SSMS)**

- **Visual Studio Code with SQL extension**

Connection string format:

```
Server=tcp:mywebappsqlserver.database.windows.net,1433;
Initial Catalog=mywebappdb;
Persist Security Info=False;
User ID=dbadmin;
Password=P@ssword123!;
MultipleActiveResultSets=False;
Encrypt=True;
TrustServerCertificate=False;
Connection Timeout=30;
```

Replace credentials with your actual values.

Step 4: Create Tables and Seed Data

Once connected, create your schema. Here's an example SQL script for a task management app:

```
CREATE TABLE Tasks (
    TaskId INT PRIMARY KEY IDENTITY(1,1),
    Title NVARCHAR(100) NOT NULL,
    Description NVARCHAR(MAX),
    DueDate DATE,
    IsComplete BIT DEFAULT 0
);

INSERT INTO Tasks (Title, Description, DueDate)
VALUES
('Buy groceries', 'Milk, Eggs, Bread', '2025-04-10'),
('Call Alice', 'Discuss project status', '2025-04-11');
```

You can run this script in the query editor of Azure Data Studio or SSMS.

Step 5: Configure Web App to Connect to Database

Update your application to connect to the database using the correct connection string. Store it in environment variables or App Settings in Azure for security.

```
az webapp config appsettings set \
  --resource-group WebAppRG \
  --name myuniquename123 \
  --settings
"SQL_CONNECTION_STRING=Server=tcp:mywebappsqlserver.database.windows
.net,1433;Initial Catalog=mywebappdb;Persist Security
Info=False;User
ID=dbadmin;Password=P@ssword123!;MultipleActiveResultSets=False;Encr
ypt=True;TrustServerCertificate=False;Connection Timeout=30;"
```

In your application code (example with Node.js using `mssql`):

```
const sql = require('mssql');

const config = {
  user: process.env.SQL_USER,
```

```
  password: process.env.SQL_PASSWORD,
  server: 'mywebappsqlserver.database.windows.net',
  database: 'mywebappdb',
  options: {
    encrypt: true,
    enableArithAbort: true
  }
};

sql.connect(config).then(pool => {
  return pool.request().query('SELECT * FROM Tasks');
}).then(result => {
  console.log(result.recordset);
}).catch(err => {
  console.error(err);
});
```

Step 6: Enable Performance Monitoring and Backups

Azure SQL Database provides automatic:

- **Performance tuning**

- **Index recommendation and creation**

- **Query performance insights**

- **Automatic backups (7 to 35 days retention)**

Enable automatic tuning:

```
az sql db tde set \
  --name mywebappdb \
  --server mywebappsqlserver \
  --resource-group DBResourceGroup \
  --status Enabled
```

Enable threat detection and auditing:

```
az sql server threat-policy update \
  --name mywebappsqlserver \
```

```
--resource-group DBResourceGroup \
--state Enabled \
--email-account-admins true \
--storage-account mylogstorage
```

Step 7: Secure Your Database

Use Azure Key Vault for Credentials

Instead of hardcoding passwords, store them in Azure Key Vault.

```
az keyvault secret set \
  --vault-name MyKeyVault \
  --name SQLConnectionString \
  --value "<your-connection-string>"
```

Configure your app to pull secrets at runtime using a managed identity.

Enable Transparent Data Encryption (TDE)

TDE is enabled by default and encrypts data at rest.

```
az sql db tde set \
  --resource-group DBResourceGroup \
  --server mywebappsqlserver \
  --name mywebappdb \
  --status Enabled
```

Step 8: Alternatives – Cosmos DB and MySQL

For non-relational or globally distributed apps, **Azure Cosmos DB** is a great choice.

```
az cosmosdb create \
  --name mycosmosdb \
  --resource-group DBResourceGroup \
  --locations regionName=eastus failoverPriority=0
```

Create a SQL API container:

```
az cosmosdb sql database create \
```

```
--account-name mycosmosdb \
--name mycosmosdbdb \
--resource-group DBResourceGroup

az cosmosdb sql container create \
--account-name mycosmosdb \
--database-name mycosmosdbdb \
--name tasks \
--partition-key-path "/userId"
```

Azure Database for MySQL is ideal for apps built with LAMP stack (Linux, Apache, MySQL, PHP).

```
az mysql flexible-server create \
--name mymysqlserver \
--resource-group DBResourceGroup \
--location eastus \
--admin-user myadmin \
--admin-password MyP@ssw0rd!
```

Step 9: Maintenance and Scaling

- Use **DTU-based** or **vCore-based** models depending on flexibility and performance requirements.

- **Scale up/down** using CLI or Portal as traffic changes.

- Use **read replicas** (for MySQL/PostgreSQL) to reduce load on primary DB.

- **Geo-replication** for high availability and DR scenarios.

Best Practices

- Avoid using admin credentials in apps—use **least privilege** principles.

- Implement **retry policies** in code to handle transient failures.

- Use **parameterized queries** or **ORMs** to avoid SQL injection.

- Regularly **audit access** and monitor logs.

- Automate schema updates using **migration tools** (e.g., Flyway, Liquibase, EF Core Migrations).

Conclusion

Setting up a simple database on Azure gives your web application the ability to persist and retrieve data reliably, securely, and at scale. By using Azure SQL Database, you gain access to a mature, enterprise-grade relational system with built-in backup, monitoring, and security features—all without managing infrastructure. As your project evolves, you can switch to or integrate with other database options like Cosmos DB or MySQL. In the next section, we'll connect your services together to complete the foundational structure of your application.

Connecting Services Together

Modern cloud applications are often composed of multiple loosely coupled services working in tandem. Once you've deployed a web app and set up a database, the next step is to **connect these services together** in a secure, scalable, and maintainable manner. Integration in Azure isn't limited to connecting just apps and databases—it extends to messaging systems, APIs, authentication services, serverless functions, monitoring tools, and more.

This section explores how to wire your services together efficiently using Azure's built-in tools and best practices. It covers connection strings, managed identities, service endpoints, environment configuration, messaging between services, securing communication, and integrating APIs.

Principles of Cloud Service Integration

When connecting cloud services, aim for:

- **Loose Coupling**: Each service should be independently deployable.

- **Clear Interfaces**: Use APIs and contracts for communication.

- **Secure Communication**: Use encryption, authentication, and scoped permissions.

- **Scalability**: Avoid bottlenecks by enabling asynchronous messaging.

- **Resilience**: Implement retries, timeouts, and circuit breakers.

These principles ensure that your system remains flexible, testable, and resilient to changes or failures in any one part.

Connecting Web App to Database

Environment Configuration

Instead of hardcoding connection details, use environment variables or Azure App Settings.

Set configuration in App Service:

```
az webapp config appsettings set \
  --resource-group WebAppRG \
  --name mywebapp123 \
  --settings \
  "SQL_SERVER=mydbserver.database.windows.net" \
  "SQL_DATABASE=mydb" \
  "SQL_USER=dbadmin" \
  "SQL_PASSWORD=P@ssw0rd123"
```

In your application code (Node.js example):

```
const config = {
  user: process.env.SQL_USER,
  password: process.env.SQL_PASSWORD,
  server: process.env.SQL_SERVER,
  database: process.env.SQL_DATABASE,
  options: { encrypt: true }
};
```

Best Practice: Store sensitive values in **Azure Key Vault** and reference them in App Settings using **Key Vault references**.

Using Managed Identities

Managed identities allow your services to authenticate to other Azure resources **without storing credentials**.

Enable Managed Identity

```
az webapp identity assign \
  --resource-group WebAppRG \
```

```
--name mywebapp123
```

This adds a system-assigned identity to your web app.

Grant Database Access

Create an Azure AD user for the web app inside SQL Server:

1. Connect using SSMS or Azure Data Studio.

2. Run the following T-SQL:

```
CREATE USER [mywebapp123] FROM EXTERNAL PROVIDER;
ALTER ROLE db_datareader ADD MEMBER [mywebapp123];
ALTER ROLE db_datawriter ADD MEMBER [mywebapp123];
```

Connect using Azure Identity SDK

In .NET (C#), use `DefaultAzureCredential`:

```
var conn = new
SqlConnection("Server=tcp:mydbserver.database.windows.net,1433;Datab
ase=mydb;Authentication=Active Directory Default;");
await conn.OpenAsync();
```

This enhances security by eliminating hardcoded secrets.

Connecting to Storage Accounts

Apps often need to connect to **Blob Storage**, **File Shares**, or **Queues**.

Set App Setting for Connection String

```
az storage account show-connection-string \
  --resource-group WebAppRG \
  --name mystorageaccount

az webapp config appsettings set \
  --resource-group WebAppRG \
  --name mywebapp123 \
  --settings "AzureWebJobsStorage=<connection-string>"
```

148 | Cloud Made Simple

Use SDKs to Interact

```
const { BlobServiceClient } = require('@azure/storage-blob');
const blobServiceClient =
BlobServiceClient.fromConnectionString(process.env.AzureWebJobsStora
ge);
```

Use Private Endpoints

For security, connect over a **Private Endpoint** to ensure traffic doesn't leave Azure's internal network.

```
az network private-endpoint create \
  --name storage-pe \
  --resource-group WebAppRG \
  --vnet-name myvnet \
  --subnet mysubnet \
  --private-connection-resource-id <storage-resource-id> \
  --group-id blob \
  --connection-name mystorageconn
```

Connecting with Messaging Services

To build scalable and decoupled systems, consider integrating messaging platforms like:

- **Azure Service Bus** (enterprise messaging)

- **Azure Event Grid** (event-based architecture)

- **Azure Queue Storage** (simple queue-based messaging)

Azure Service Bus Example

Create a namespace and queue:

```
az servicebus namespace create --resource-group WebAppRG --name
mybusnamespace --location eastus
az servicebus queue create --resource-group WebAppRG --namespace-
name mybusnamespace --name orders
```

Set connection string in web app:

```
az servicebus namespace authorization-rule keys list \
```

```
--resource-group WebAppRG \
--namespace-name mybusnamespace \
--name RootManageSharedAccessKey
```

Use SDK in app:

```
const { ServiceBusClient } = require("@azure/service-bus");
const client = new
ServiceBusClient(process.env.SERVICEBUS_CONNECTION_STRING);
const sender = client.createSender("orders");

await sender.sendMessages({ body: "Order #123" });
```

Connecting to Azure Functions

Use Azure Functions to offload asynchronous or background tasks such as:

- Sending emails

- Processing images

- Updating analytics

Trigger Functions via:

- **HTTP requests**

- **Service Bus messages**

- **Storage changes**

Create Function App

```
az functionapp create \
  --resource-group WebAppRG \
  --consumption-plan-location eastus \
  --runtime node \
  --functions-version 4 \
  --name myfunctionapp \
  --storage-account mystorage
```

Connect Web App to Function

Use Azure App Settings to define the Function endpoint:

```
az webapp config appsettings set \
  --resource-group WebAppRG \
  --name mywebapp123 \
  --settings
"FUNCTION_URL=https://myfunctionapp.azurewebsites.net/api/processord
er"
```

Call from your app:

```
await fetch(process.env.FUNCTION_URL, {
  method: 'POST',
  body: JSON.stringify({ orderId: 123 })
});
```

Integrating APIs with API Management

Use **Azure API Management (APIM)** to expose your services securely, apply rate limiting, and add custom policies.

Create APIM Instance

```
az apim create \
  --name myapim \
  --resource-group WebAppRG \
  --publisher-email admin@contoso.com \
  --publisher-name Contoso
```

Add an API Backend

You can import OpenAPI (Swagger) definitions or add an HTTP backend manually. Once configured, route your frontend traffic through APIM.

Benefits:

- Security with API keys and OAuth

- Rate limiting and quotas

- Developer portal for documentation

- Request/response transformation

Secure Communication Between Services

Use TLS Everywhere

Azure services communicate over HTTPS by default. Avoid non-encrypted connections unless inside a secure, private network.

Isolate Traffic with Virtual Networks

Place dependent services (e.g., SQL, Storage, Redis) inside a **Virtual Network (VNet)** and access via **Private Endpoints**.

Use **VNet Integration** for Web Apps:

```
az webapp vnet-integration add \
  --name mywebapp123 \
  --resource-group WebAppRG \
  --vnet myvnet \
  --subnet appsubnet
```

Monitor Connected Services

Use **Azure Monitor**, **Application Insights**, and **Log Analytics** to:

- Trace requests across services

- Monitor dependencies and response times

- Diagnose failures

Enable dependency tracking in Application Insights to view how services interact.

In .NET:

```
services.AddApplicationInsightsTelemetry();
```

In Node.js:

```
const appInsights = require("applicationinsights");
appInsights.setup().start();
```

Best Practices

- Use **Managed Identities** for secure service-to-service communication.

- Store configuration and secrets in **App Settings** and **Key Vault**.

- Use **Azure Event Grid or Service Bus** for scalable messaging.

- Secure external APIs with **API Management**.

- Use **Health Probes** and **Retry Policies** to improve resilience.

- Log and monitor **end-to-end workflows**.

Conclusion

Connecting services together is where your cloud architecture comes alive. Azure provides robust and secure ways to stitch together everything from databases and storage, to APIs and background workers. By applying best practices such as using managed identities, private networking, and asynchronous messaging, you can build a system that's not only functional but also secure, scalable, and resilient. In the next section, we'll learn how to monitor and manage these resources to ensure everything runs smoothly in production.

Monitoring and Managing Resources

Once your Azure application is live and serving users, your responsibilities extend beyond deployment. Ensuring consistent performance, security, cost-efficiency, and system health requires continuous monitoring and proactive management of your Azure resources. Fortunately, Azure offers a comprehensive suite of tools for observability, diagnostics, alerting, automation, and resource optimization.

This section dives deep into how to monitor, manage, and maintain your deployed services and infrastructure using tools such as **Azure Monitor**, **Application Insights**, **Log Analytics**, **Azure Advisor**, and **Automation**. It also covers organizing resources with tags and resource groups, and setting up governance for large-scale environments.

Why Monitoring and Management Matter

Visibility, **insight**, and **actionability** are critical pillars of cloud operations. Monitoring isn't just about detecting problems—it's about **preventing outages, identifying bottlenecks,**

and **managing costs** effectively. With dynamic workloads, being reactive is not enough; successful teams use monitoring to enable predictive and preventive operations.

Key goals of monitoring and management:

- Detect anomalies before users are impacted

- Track usage patterns and performance trends

- Maintain compliance and security posture

- Optimize resource utilization

- Automate repetitive tasks

Azure Monitor: The Foundation of Observability

Azure Monitor is the unified platform for collecting, analyzing, and acting on telemetry data from your Azure and hybrid environments.

What Azure Monitor Tracks:

- **Metrics**: Numeric performance data like CPU usage, memory, disk I/O

- **Logs**: Structured data from activity logs, diagnostics, and custom sources

- **Alerts**: Rules triggered when conditions are met

- **Dashboards**: Customizable views of key metrics

- **Workbooks**: Interactive reports for deeper analysis

Enabling Azure Monitor

Azure Monitor is enabled by default for many services. You can enhance it by configuring diagnostics and integrating with other tools:

```
az monitor diagnostic-settings create \
  --resource
/subscriptions/<subId>/resourceGroups/WebAppRG/providers/Microsoft.W
eb/sites/mywebapp \
  --name EnableDiagnostics \
  --workspace <logAnalyticsWorkspaceId> \
  --logs '[{"category": "AppServiceHTTPLogs","enabled": true}]'
```

This example routes logs from an App Service to a Log Analytics workspace.

Application Insights: Deep Insights for Applications

Application Insights is designed to monitor live web applications, providing performance telemetry, user behavior insights, and diagnostics.

Key Features:

- Request rates, durations, and failure rates

- Exception and stack trace analysis

- Live metrics stream

- Custom telemetry and tracking

- Dependency tracking (e.g., calls to databases, APIs)

Adding Application Insights to a Web App

1. Create an Application Insights resource:

```
az monitor app-insights component create \
  --app MyAppInsights \
  --location eastus \
  --resource-group WebAppRG \
  --application-type web
```

2. Link it to your web app:

```
az webapp config appsettings set \
  --resource-group WebAppRG \
  --name mywebapp \
  --settings APPINSIGHTS_INSTRUMENTATIONKEY=<instrumentation-key>
```

3. In your code (Node.js example):

```
const appInsights = require("applicationinsights");
appInsights.setup().start();
```

You can now view live metrics, failure traces, and user session data directly in the Azure Portal.

Log Analytics: Advanced Querying and Analysis

Log Analytics allows you to query telemetry data using a powerful language called **Kusto Query Language (KQL)**.

Example: Identify high-latency HTTP requests:

```
requests
| where duration > 1000
| project timestamp, name, duration, resultCode
| sort by duration desc
```

Example: Count failed logins:

```
SigninLogs
| where ResultType != 0
| summarize count() by UserPrincipalName
```

These queries help identify performance issues and suspicious activity quickly.

Setting Up Alerts

Create alerts to be notified about issues proactively.

Example: Alert when CPU usage exceeds 80%

```
az monitor metrics alert create \
  --name HighCPU \
  --resource-group WebAppRG \
  --scopes
/subscriptions/<subId>/resourceGroups/WebAppRG/providers/Microsoft.W
eb/sites/mywebapp \
  --condition "avg Percentage CPU > 80" \
  --description "Alert for high CPU usage" \
```

```
--action-group myAlertGroup
```

Create an action group to send emails or run automation:

```
az monitor action-group create \
  --name myAlertGroup \
  --resource-group WebAppRG \
  --short-name alertgrp \
  --email-receivers name=OpsTeam email=ops@example.com
```

Azure Advisor: Intelligent Recommendations

Azure Advisor provides personalized best practices for your subscriptions in the following areas:

- High availability
- Security
- Performance
- Cost
- Operational Excellence

Access Azure Advisor via the portal or CLI:

```
az advisor recommendation list --output table
```

You'll get suggestions like resizing underutilized VMs, enabling geo-redundancy, or configuring missing backups.

Automation and Scheduling

Repetitive tasks like backups, scale operations, or resource cleanup can be automated using **Azure Automation** or **Logic Apps**.

Azure Automation Example

Create a runbook to shut down VMs every night:

```
Stop-AzVM -Name myVM -ResourceGroupName WebAppRG -Force
```

Schedule it via **Automation Account > Runbooks > Schedules**.

Logic Apps Example

Automatically notify on Slack when a VM starts:

1. Trigger: Azure Event (VM start)

2. Action: Send Slack message

Managing Resources with Tags and Groups

Organizing resources helps with automation, access control, and billing.

Tagging Resources

```
az resource tag \
  --resource-id
"/subscriptions/<subId>/resourceGroups/WebAppRG/providers/Microsoft.
Web/sites/mywebapp" \
  --tags Environment=Production Owner=DevTeam Project=TodoApp
```

Using Resource Groups

Group resources that share a lifecycle (e.g., dev vs prod). Deleting a resource group deletes all contained resources.

```
az group create --name ProdRG --location westeurope
az group delete --name OldRG --yes --no-wait
```

Scaling Resources Dynamically

Monitor load patterns and scale resources automatically.

App Service Autoscale

```
az monitor autoscale create \
  --resource-group WebAppRG \
  --resource WebAppPlan \
  --resource-type Microsoft.Web/serverfarms \
```

```
--name AutoScaleApp \
--min-count 1 \
--max-count 5 \
--count 2
```

Add a rule to scale out when CPU exceeds 70%:

```
az monitor autoscale rule create \
  --resource-group WebAppRG \
  --autoscale-name AutoScaleApp \
  --condition "Percentage CPU > 70 avg 5m" \
  --scale out 1
```

Auditing and Compliance

For regulated workloads, Azure supports **auditing**, **logging**, and **compliance reporting**.

Enable activity logs for tracking resource changes:

```
az monitor activity-log list --resource-group WebAppRG
```

Integrate with **Microsoft Defender for Cloud** for:

- Threat detection

- Security recommendations

- Regulatory compliance reports

Disaster Recovery and Backups

Ensure recovery plans are in place for key resources:

- **App Service**: Enable daily backups

- **SQL Database**: Configure geo-replication and restore points

- **Storage Accounts**: Use soft delete and versioning

Enable backup for App Service:

```
az webapp config backup create \
  --resource-group WebAppRG \
  --webapp-name mywebapp \
  --container-url <sas-enabled-storage-url>
```

Best Practices

- Enable **Application Insights** in every app

- Set up **alerts** for all mission-critical resources

- Use **autoscale** and **scheduling** to manage costs

- Tag every resource with purpose, environment, and owner

- Periodically review **Azure Advisor** recommendations

- Use **Key Vault** for all secrets and credentials

- Monitor **Service Health** for regional Azure issues

Conclusion

Effective monitoring and management are not optional—they are the lifeblood of running successful applications in the cloud. Azure provides a rich set of tools to help you keep your services healthy, secure, and cost-efficient. By actively observing application behavior, analyzing telemetry, setting up smart alerts, automating maintenance, and implementing governance policies, you ensure your application is not only functional but enterprise-ready. In the following chapter, we'll shift focus to securing your environment—because strong identity, access, and data protections are crucial as your cloud usage scales.

Chapter 5: Securing Your Azure Environment

Fundamentals of Azure Security

As organizations move workloads and data into the cloud, ensuring the security of cloud-based environments becomes a top priority. Microsoft Azure, as a leading cloud provider, offers a robust and comprehensive set of tools, features, and best practices to help organizations safeguard their assets. Understanding the foundational principles of Azure security is essential for implementing a secure and compliant environment from the outset.

The Shared Responsibility Model

Security in the cloud is a shared responsibility between Microsoft and the customer. Microsoft is responsible for the security **of** the cloud, including physical infrastructure, network controls, and foundational services. The customer, on the other hand, is responsible for security **in** the cloud—meaning they must configure and manage identity, data, access, and other application-level concerns.

Understanding this division is critical:

- **Microsoft's Responsibility**:

    - Physical data centers

    - Host infrastructure

    - Network infrastructure

    - Foundational services (compute, storage, networking)

- **Customer's Responsibility**:

    - Data governance and rights management

    - Identity and access management

    - Application security

    - Network controls (e.g., Network Security Groups)

    - Endpoint protection

    - Account and authentication settings

Azure Security Center

Azure Security Center (now integrated into Microsoft Defender for Cloud) is a unified infrastructure security management system that strengthens the security posture of your data centers. It provides advanced threat protection across hybrid cloud workloads.

Key features include:

- **Security posture management**: Assessing and visualizing your current security state with recommendations.

- **Threat protection**: Detecting and responding to threats using advanced analytics.

- **Regulatory compliance**: Continuous assessments based on built-in standards (e.g., ISO 27001, NIST, PCI-DSS).

You can access Azure Security Center directly from the Azure Portal. Enabling enhanced security features provides additional insight and automation capabilities.

Example: Enabling Azure Defender for a subscription via PowerShell:

```
Set-AzSecurityPricing -Name "default" -PricingTier "Standard"
```

Network Security Basics

Network security is foundational in protecting resources hosted in Azure. Azure provides multiple layers of network security to help isolate and control traffic.

Virtual Network (VNet) Segmentation

- Use VNets to logically isolate workloads.

- Create subnets within a VNet to separate services.

- Implement NSGs (Network Security Groups) to control inbound and outbound traffic.

```
{
  "name": "AllowWebTraffic",
  "properties": {
    "priority": 100,
    "direction": "Inbound",
    "access": "Allow",
    "protocol": "Tcp",
    "sourcePortRange": "*",
    "destinationPortRange": "80",
```

```
  "sourceAddressPrefix": "*",
  "destinationAddressPrefix": "*"
  }
}
```

☐Azure Firewall and DDoS Protection

- Use **Azure Firewall** for stateful inspection, logging, and filtering of traffic.

- Enable **Azure DDoS Protection Standard** to guard against distributed denial-of-service attacks.

Identity and Access Management (IAM)

Properly managing identity and access is crucial to prevent unauthorized access.

Azure Active Directory (Azure AD)

Azure AD is Microsoft's cloud-based identity and access management service, which enables:

- **Single sign-on (SSO)** across applications

- **Multi-factor authentication (MFA)**

- Conditional access policies

- Integration with on-premises Active Directory

MFA Enforcement

Requiring multiple forms of authentication reduces the risk of credential theft.

Example: Enforcing MFA for all users using Azure AD Conditional Access:

1. Go to Azure AD → Security → Conditional Access

2. Create a new policy

3. Assign it to "All Users"

4. Under "Grant", select "Require multi-factor authentication"

5. Enable and save the policy

Role-Based Access Control (RBAC)

RBAC allows fine-grained access management for Azure resources.

- Assign users, groups, or managed identities to built-in or custom roles.

- Scope assignments to a **subscription**, **resource group**, or **individual resource**.

Example: Assign the Reader role to a user for a resource group:

```
az role assignment create --assignee <userPrincipalName> --role
Reader --resource-group MyResourceGroup
```

Data Protection

Encryption at Rest

Azure ensures that data is encrypted at rest using Storage Service Encryption (SSE). For added control, you can use **Customer-Managed Keys (CMK)** instead of **Microsoft-Managed Keys**.

Azure Disk Encryption example using PowerShell:

```
Set-AzVMDiskEncryptionExtension -ResourceGroupName "MyRG" `
  -VMName "MyVM" `
  -DiskEncryptionKeyVaultUrl $keyVaultUrl `
  -DiskEncryptionKeyVaultId $keyVaultId
```

Encryption in Transit

All data transmitted between Azure data centers or to clients uses TLS (Transport Layer Security). Enforcing HTTPS on web apps and APIs is critical.

To enforce HTTPS in an Azure App Service:

1. Go to your App Service → TLS/SSL settings

2. Set "HTTPS Only" to On

Logging and Monitoring

Continuous monitoring is critical to detect suspicious activity and diagnose issues.

Azure Monitor and Log Analytics

Azure Monitor collects and analyzes telemetry data from your applications and infrastructure.

- **Activity logs** track control-plane operations (e.g., resource creation)

- **Diagnostic logs** record resource-specific activities (e.g., VM performance)

- Use **Log Analytics** to query and analyze logs.

Sample Kusto Query Language (KQL) query:

```
SecurityEvent
| where TimeGenerated > ago(1d)
| where EventID == 4625
| summarize FailedLogins = count() by Account
```

Azure Policy

Azure Policy enforces organizational standards and assesses compliance at scale. For example, you can require all resources to be tagged or deny deployments to unapproved regions.

Example policy to enforce tagging:

```
{
  "if": {
    "field": "[concat('tags[', parameters('tagName'), ']')]",
    "exists": "false"
  },
  "then": {
    "effect": "deny"
  }
}
```

Secure DevOps Practices

Security should be integrated into every stage of the DevOps lifecycle.

- Use **Azure DevOps** or **GitHub Actions** with secure pipelines.

- Scan code with tools like **Microsoft Defender for DevOps**.

- Store secrets securely in **Azure Key Vault**, not in code.

Example: Accessing a secret from Azure Key Vault in a CI pipeline:

```
- task: AzureKeyVault@2
  inputs:
```

```
connectedServiceName: '<service-connection>'
keyVaultName: '<key-vault-name>'
secretsFilter: 'MySecret'
```

☐Regulatory Compliance and Trust

Azure provides over **100 compliance offerings**, making it suitable for regulated industries such as finance and healthcare.

You can access compliance documentation through the **Microsoft Trust Center** and **Compliance Manager**, which helps assess and manage compliance postures.

Compliance Manager helps you:

- Track standards like GDPR, ISO 27001, and HIPAA.

- Get recommendations and actionable insights.

- Assign improvement actions to team members.

Summary

Securing your Azure environment involves more than enabling a few features. It requires a comprehensive, layered approach—from controlling identity and access to encrypting data and proactively monitoring your cloud environment.

Key takeaways include:

- Understand and act on the Shared Responsibility Model.

- Use Azure-native tools like Security Center and Azure Policy.

- Enforce MFA, implement RBAC, and configure NSGs and Firewalls.

- Encrypt data at rest and in transit.

- Monitor continuously with Azure Monitor and Defender for Cloud.

- Build security into DevOps practices.

- Stay compliant with regulatory standards.

Building a secure foundation in Azure is a continuous journey—one that starts with understanding and applying these fundamental concepts consistently across your cloud infrastructure.

Role-Based Access Control (RBAC)

Role-Based Access Control (RBAC) is a fundamental security feature in Microsoft Azure that allows you to manage who has access to Azure resources, what they can do with those resources, and what areas they have access to. RBAC enables organizations to implement the principle of least privilege by assigning only the necessary permissions users need to perform their tasks.

RBAC is built on three core components:

- **Security Principal** – The user, group, service principal, or managed identity requesting access to Azure resources.

- **Role Definition** – A collection of permissions that determine what actions can be performed, such as read, write, or delete.

- **Scope** – The set of resources the access applies to, such as a subscription, resource group, or specific resource.

By combining these elements, RBAC offers a highly flexible and granular access control mechanism that can be scaled to meet enterprise-level security requirements.

Why Use RBAC?

RBAC helps:

- **Limit access based on roles**, not individuals, simplifying permission management.

- **Reduce the risk** of accidental or malicious operations.

- **Enable delegation**, allowing resource owners to manage their own assets.

- **Improve auditing**, providing clear tracking of who did what.

Built-in and Custom Roles

Azure provides over 70 built-in roles, each designed for common tasks. Some examples include:

- **Owner** – Full access to all resources, including the right to delegate access.

- **Contributor** – Can create and manage all types of Azure resources but cannot grant access.

- **Reader** – Can view existing resources but cannot make changes.

- **User Access Administrator** – Can manage user access to Azure resources.

If built-in roles do not meet your specific needs, you can create custom roles with precisely defined permissions.

Example of a custom role that grants read-only access to storage accounts:

```
{
  "Name": "Custom Storage Reader",
  "IsCustom": true,
  "Description": "Can read storage account information",
  "Actions": [
    "Microsoft.Storage/storageAccounts/read"
  ],
  "NotActions": [],
  "AssignableScopes": [
    "/subscriptions/xxxxxxxx-xxxx-xxxx-xxxx-xxxxxxxxxxxx"
  ]
}
```

To create this custom role, use PowerShell or the Azure CLI:

```
az role definition create --role-definition customStorageReader.json
```

Understanding Scope

In RBAC, scope determines where the access applies. Permissions can be granted at four levels:

1. **Management Group**
2. **Subscription**
3. **Resource Group**
4. **Resource**

The broader the scope, the more access the user has. For example, assigning the "Contributor" role at the subscription level allows changes across all resources in that subscription.

It's a best practice to assign roles at the **lowest possible scope** required for a task.

Assigning Roles

You can assign roles via the Azure Portal, CLI, PowerShell, or through templates.

Assigning a Role via the Azure Portal

1. Navigate to the resource (e.g., Resource Group).

2. Click **Access control (IAM)**.

3. Click **+ Add** → **Add role assignment**.

4. Select the role (e.g., Contributor).

5. Select the user, group, or service principal.

6. Click **Save**.

Assigning a Role Using Azure CLI

```
az role assignment create \
  --assignee user@domain.com \
  --role "Reader" \
  --scope /subscriptions/xxxx-xxxx-xxxx-
xxxx/resourceGroups/MyResourceGroup
```

RBAC for Resource Hierarchies

Because Azure resources are organized hierarchically, permissions are inherited by default. If you assign a role at the subscription level, it automatically applies to all resource groups and resources within that subscription.

You can override inherited permissions by using **Deny Assignments** (via Azure Blueprints or Policy), but RBAC itself does not support explicit deny rules.

Managed Identities and RBAC

Managed identities provide Azure services with an automatically managed identity in Azure AD. This identity can be used to authenticate to services that support Azure AD authentication.

You can grant a managed identity access to resources using RBAC, avoiding the need to manage credentials.

Example: Assigning a role to a managed identity:

```
az role assignment create \
  --assignee-object-id <object-id-of-managed-identity> \
  --role "Reader" \
  --scope /subscriptions/<subscription-id>/resourceGroups/<group-
name>
```

Best Practices for RBAC

1. **Use groups instead of individual users** for role assignments to simplify management.

2. **Grant least privilege**—assign only the permissions required to perform the job.

3. **Audit regularly** to ensure permissions remain appropriate over time.

4. **Remove unused role assignments** and users who no longer need access.

5. **Use custom roles** to tailor access precisely, but avoid unnecessary complexity.

6. **Leverage Azure AD PIM (Privileged Identity Management)** for just-in-time role elevation.

RBAC vs. Azure Policy

It's important not to confuse RBAC with Azure Policy. RBAC governs **what actions** a user can perform, while Azure Policy governs **what resources** can be created and how those resources are configured.

RBAC = *Who can do what?*

Azure Policy = *What is allowed to exist?*

Both tools are complementary and can be used together to enforce security and governance.

Auditing Role Assignments

Use Azure Monitor and Activity Logs to track role assignments and changes. This helps with compliance and forensic analysis.

Example KQL query to identify RBAC changes:

```
AuditLogs
| where ActivityDisplayName == "Add member to role"
| project TimeGenerated, InitiatedBy, TargetResources
```

Automating Role Assignments with ARM/Bicep

You can automate role assignments using templates for repeatable deployments.

Bicep Example:

```
resource roleAssignment
'Microsoft.Authorization/roleAssignments@2020-04-01-preview' = {
  name: guid(resourceGroup().id, 'reader-role')
  properties: {
    roleDefinitionId:
subscriptionResourceId('Microsoft.Authorization/roleDefinitions',
'acdd72a7-3385-48ef-bd42-f606fba81ae7') // Reader
    principalId: '<user-object-id>'
    scope: resourceGroup().id
  }
}
```

Troubleshooting RBAC Issues

If a user reports that they cannot access a resource:

- Check that they have the correct **role**.

- Confirm the **scope** is correct.

- Validate the user is in the correct **Azure AD tenant**.

- Look at **Activity Logs** for changes or removals of permissions.

You can also use the **Access Review** tool in Azure AD to conduct periodic audits of access levels and make access reviews easier for larger organizations.

Summary

Role-Based Access Control is a cornerstone of Azure's identity and access management strategy. By understanding and applying RBAC properly, organizations can significantly reduce risk, support compliance efforts, and operate more efficiently. Whether you are assigning built-in roles, designing custom ones, or managing permissions programmatically, RBAC gives you the control and granularity needed to secure Azure environments effectively.

Key Points:

- RBAC governs permissions through role assignments scoped to resources.

- Use built-in roles where possible, and custom roles when necessary.

- Always follow the principle of least privilege.

- Regularly audit role assignments and remove unused permissions.

- Combine RBAC with other tools like Azure Policy and PIM for a robust governance strategy.

RBAC is not just a feature—it is a framework for secure operations in the cloud. Mastering it is essential for every Azure administrator, architect, and developer.

Encryption and Compliance Tools

In a cloud-first world, securing data at every stage—at rest, in transit, and during processing—is paramount. Encryption is one of the most powerful techniques to protect sensitive information and enforce privacy. Azure provides a robust suite of encryption technologies and compliance tools that empower organizations to meet regulatory requirements, industry standards, and internal security policies.

Encryption in Azure is applied across a wide spectrum of services and use cases. This section explores the key components of Azure's encryption framework and outlines how compliance tools help ensure that environments adhere to necessary standards.

Types of Encryption in Azure

Azure supports encryption in several contexts:

- **Encryption at rest**: Protects stored data from unauthorized access.

- **Encryption in transit**: Secures data while being transferred.

- **Encryption in use**: Protects data during computation (e.g., confidential computing).

- **Application-level encryption**: Encrypts data at the application layer using custom logic.

Understanding how these mechanisms operate individually and together is essential for designing a secure architecture.

Encryption at Rest

Azure automatically encrypts data before persisting it to disk and decrypts it when accessed by an authorized user or application. The encryption is transparent and built into many services.

Server-Side Encryption (SSE)

Most Azure services offer Server-Side Encryption, where Azure handles key management and encryption processes.

- **Storage Accounts**: Data is encrypted using AES-256.

- **Azure SQL Database**: Transparent Data Encryption (TDE) is enabled by default.

- **Azure Virtual Machines**: Disks are encrypted using Storage Service Encryption (SSE).

Customer-Managed Keys (CMK)

By default, Microsoft manages the encryption keys. However, for organizations requiring greater control, Azure allows customers to use their own keys, managed in **Azure Key Vault** or **Azure Key Vault Managed HSM**.

Benefits of CMK:

- Greater control over key lifecycle

- Support for revocation and rotation

- Meets regulatory or organizational compliance

Example: Enabling CMK on a storage account

```
az keyvault key create --vault-name MyKeyVault --name MyKey --
protection software

az storage account update \
  --name mystorageaccount \
  --resource-group MyResourceGroup \
  --encryption-key-source Microsoft.Keyvault \
  --encryption-key-vault MyKeyVault \
  --encryption-key-name MyKey
```

Disk Encryption

Azure Disk Encryption uses BitLocker (Windows) and DM-Crypt (Linux) to encrypt OS and data disks of Azure VMs.

To enable Disk Encryption using PowerShell:

```
Set-AzVMDiskEncryptionExtension -ResourceGroupName "MyRG" `
  -VMName "MyVM" `
  -DiskEncryptionKeyVaultUrl $keyVaultUrl `
  -DiskEncryptionKeyVaultId $keyVaultId
```

Disk Encryption is especially important for scenarios requiring compliance with standards such as HIPAA or FedRAMP.

Encryption in Transit

Azure uses industry-standard protocols such as **TLS 1.2+** to secure data in transit.

Services where encryption in transit is enforced:

- Azure Storage

- Azure SQL Database

- Azure Kubernetes Service (AKS)

- Azure App Service

You can enforce HTTPS-only traffic for services like App Services:

```
az webapp update --name mywebapp --resource-group MyRG --https-only
true
```

Best Practices:

- Always enforce HTTPS for web applications.

- Use Azure Front Door or Application Gateway with WAF for secure traffic routing.

- Use IPsec or VPN for on-prem to cloud secure communication.

Encryption in Use

Encryption in use protects data while it is being processed in memory. Azure achieves this using **Confidential Computing**—a model that leverages **Trusted Execution Environments (TEEs)**.

Use cases include:

- Secure multi-party computation

- Protecting intellectual property

- Processing sensitive healthcare or financial data

Confidential VMs in Azure (DCsv2-series) support Intel SGX, enabling secure enclaves for code and data execution.

You can deploy a confidential VM as follows:

```
az vm create \
  --name confidentialVM \
  --resource-group MyRG \
  --image ConfidentialOS \
  --size Standard_DC2s_v2
```

Azure Key Vault

Azure Key Vault is the cornerstone of managing secrets, keys, and certificates. It acts as a secure storage and access management service for sensitive data.

Key Features:

- Stores symmetric and asymmetric keys

- Manages secrets (e.g., connection strings, API keys)

- Integrates with HSMs (Hardware Security Modules)

- Supports role-based access with Azure RBAC

- Provides audit logging through Azure Monitor

Example: Storing a secret

```
az keyvault secret set --vault-name MyKeyVault --name "DbPassword" --value "MyP@ssword123"
```

Key Vault can be integrated directly with services like App Services and Azure Functions, allowing secrets to be retrieved at runtime without being stored in code.

Azure Confidential Ledger

For immutable and tamper-proof data recording, Azure Confidential Ledger provides a decentralized and cryptographically verifiable log. This is ideal for scenarios like audit trails, compliance records, or supply chain verifications.

Built on a trusted execution environment, it ensures that data cannot be altered, even by administrators.

Azure Purview (Microsoft Purview)

Microsoft Purview helps with data governance and compliance by enabling:

- **Data discovery and classification**

- **Mapping of sensitive information**

- **Data lineage tracking**

It integrates with Azure Information Protection and Microsoft 365 Compliance tools to classify and label data automatically.

Purview helps you answer:

- Where is my sensitive data?

- Who has access to it?

- How is it being used?

Compliance Manager

Azure Compliance Manager helps manage compliance across Azure and Microsoft 365 environments. It provides:

- Prebuilt assessment templates for regulations like **GDPR**, **ISO 27001**, **HIPAA**, and **NIST**

- Score-based tracking of compliance posture

- Recommended improvement actions

- Workflow assignment to team members

This tool is especially valuable in industries with strict auditing requirements.

To access it:

1. Go to Microsoft Purview portal

2. Navigate to **Compliance Manager**

3. Choose an assessment template (e.g., GDPR)

4. Review improvement actions and assign owners

Azure Policy for Compliance

Azure Policy allows organizations to enforce rules across resources to ensure compliance. For example:

- Enforce encryption at rest

- Require specific tags for cost tracking

- Deny unapproved SKUs or regions

Example: Policy to enforce encryption

```
{
  "if": {
    "field":
"Microsoft.Storage/storageAccounts/encryption.services.blob.enabled"
,
    "equals": "false"
  },
  "then": {
    "effect": "deny"
  }
}
```

Blueprints for Governance

Azure Blueprints enable teams to define and repeat a set of Azure resources, policies, and role assignments to enforce standards.

A blueprint can include:

- Resource templates (ARM or Bicep)

- Role assignments

- Policy assignments

- Resource groups

This is particularly useful in enterprise environments for regulatory alignment.

Logging and Auditing

Logs are vital for tracking access to keys and encrypted resources. Azure offers:

- **Azure Monitor Logs**

- **Azure Activity Logs**

- **Key Vault Diagnostic Logs**

Use KQL (Kusto Query Language) to query and monitor suspicious activity:

```
AzureDiagnostics
| where ResourceType == "VAULT"
| where OperationName == "SecretGet"
| summarize Count = count() by Identity
```

Best Practices for Encryption and Compliance

1. **Always use encryption at rest and in transit**—don't rely on defaults alone.

2. **Use customer-managed keys** for higher control and revocation capabilities.

3. **Centralize key management** using Azure Key Vault.

4. **Enforce HTTPS and TLS across services**.

5. **Enable disk encryption** for all production VMs.

6. **Integrate logging and alerting** for all key operations.

7. **Run regular compliance assessments** via Compliance Manager.

8. **Use Azure Policy and Blueprints** to standardize environments.

Summary

Encryption and compliance in Azure form the bedrock of a secure and regulated cloud architecture. From native encryption mechanisms to customer-managed key strategies, Azure equips teams with the tools necessary to protect data across its entire lifecycle.

Equally important, the array of compliance tools like Azure Policy, Microsoft Purview, and Compliance Manager help ensure that environments meet external regulations and internal governance frameworks. These tools provide transparency, accountability, and auditability— essential qualities for building trust in cloud operations.

Whether you're storing confidential data, managing access to encryption keys, or enforcing regulatory standards, Azure offers an integrated, enterprise-grade approach that simplifies complex security requirements without compromising on control or flexibility.

Best Practices for Secure Cloud Deployments

Designing and operating secure cloud deployments in Azure is not a one-time event—it is an ongoing process of planning, implementation, auditing, and continuous improvement. While Microsoft Azure provides a robust security foundation, the security of your environment depends heavily on how you configure and maintain your cloud resources.

This section presents a comprehensive overview of best practices for secure cloud deployments in Azure. It covers foundational principles, configuration strategies, tools, policies, and real-world recommendations to help organizations harden their cloud environments and defend against evolving threats.

Principle of Least Privilege

The **Principle of Least Privilege (PoLP)** is the practice of granting users and services the minimum level of access required to perform their tasks.

Recommendations:

- Use **Role-Based Access Control (RBAC)** to define specific permissions.

- Assign roles at the **lowest possible scope** (resource vs. subscription).

- Regularly audit roles and access to eliminate unnecessary permissions.

- Avoid using the **Owner** role unless absolutely necessary.

- Prefer **group-based access** over individual user assignments.

Example:

```
az role assignment create \
```

```
--assignee user@example.com \
--role "Reader" \
--scope /subscriptions/xxxx-xxxx-xxxx/resourceGroups/myRG
```

Secure Identity and Access Management

Identity is the new perimeter in the cloud era. Mismanaged identity and access controls are a leading cause of security incidents.

Best Practices:

- **Enforce Multi-Factor Authentication (MFA)** for all users.

- Enable **Conditional Access Policies** to control access based on location, device, or risk level.

- Use **Azure Active Directory (Azure AD)** with identity protection features enabled.

- Implement **Privileged Identity Management (PIM)** to provide just-in-time access for admin roles.

- Use **Managed Identities** for applications to avoid hardcoded secrets.

Enforcing MFA for all users:

1. Azure AD → Security → Conditional Access

2. New Policy → Assign to "All Users"

3. Grant → "Require Multi-Factor Authentication"

Secure Network Design

A well-segmented and monitored network is critical to preventing lateral movement by attackers.

Strategies:

- Segment environments using **Virtual Networks (VNets)** and **subnets**.

- Use **Network Security Groups (NSGs)** to control traffic to/from subnets.

- Deploy **Azure Firewall** or **Network Virtual Appliances (NVAs)** for advanced traffic inspection.

- Enable **DDoS Protection Standard** to guard against volumetric attacks.

- Use **Private Endpoints** to access services securely over the Azure backbone.

Example NSG Rule (JSON):

```json
{
  "name": "AllowHTTP",
  "properties": {
    "priority": 100,
    "access": "Allow",
    "direction": "Inbound",
    "protocol": "Tcp",
    "sourceAddressPrefix": "*",
    "destinationPortRange": "80",
    "destinationAddressPrefix": "*",
    "sourcePortRange": "*"
  }
}
```

Encryption Everywhere

Data must be encrypted during storage, transmission, and processing to maintain confidentiality and compliance.

Recommendations:

- Ensure **encryption at rest** is enabled using **Azure Storage Encryption** or **Disk Encryption**.

- Use **customer-managed keys** stored in **Azure Key Vault** for increased control.

- Force **HTTPS** across all public endpoints.

- Encrypt **data in transit** using TLS 1.2 or higher.

- Leverage **confidential computing** and **Trusted Execution Environments (TEEs)** for encryption in use.

Force HTTPS on an Azure Web App:

```
az webapp update --name myApp --resource-group myRG --https-only
true
```

Secure DevOps (DevSecOps)

Incorporating security into every stage of the development lifecycle is critical for early detection and remediation.

Best Practices:

- Integrate **static code analysis (SAST)** into CI/CD pipelines.

- Use **Azure DevOps** or **GitHub Actions** with built-in security scanning.

- Store secrets in **Azure Key Vault**, not in code repositories.

- Scan container images using **Microsoft Defender for Containers**.

- Enable **infrastructure-as-code scanning** using tools like **Terraform Sentinel**, **Checkov**, or **bicep linter**.

Azure Key Vault in GitHub Actions:

```
- uses: azure/keyvault-secrets@v1
  with:
    keyvault: "myKeyVault"
    secrets: "dbPassword"
```

Threat Detection and Monitoring

You can't secure what you can't see. Continuous visibility into the environment helps detect misconfigurations, threats, and anomalies.

Key Tools:

- **Microsoft Defender for Cloud** for workload protection and recommendations.

- **Azure Monitor** for metrics and logs.

- **Log Analytics** for querying security events.

- **Azure Sentinel** for SIEM and threat detection across environments.

Example KQL Query to Detect Failed Logins:

```
SecurityEvent
| where TimeGenerated > ago(1d)
| where EventID == 4625
| summarize FailedAttempts = count() by Account
```

Patching and Vulnerability Management

Unpatched systems are a common attack vector. Azure provides several tools to help manage and remediate vulnerabilities.

Recommendations:

- Enable **automatic OS patching** on VMs and App Services.

- Use **Azure Automation** or **Update Management Center** for centralized patch orchestration.

- Monitor security baseline compliance using **Microsoft Defender for Servers**.

- Scan container images with **ACR Tasks** or **Microsoft Defender for Containers**.

Resource Tagging and Inventory

Proper tagging and resource tracking are important for cost control, access management, and auditing.

Tag Examples:

```
{
  "Environment": "Production",
  "Owner": "frahaan@company.com",
  "Compliance": "HIPAA",
  "CostCenter": "1001"
}
```

Enforce tagging with Azure Policy:

```
{
  "if": {
    "field": "tags.Environment",
    "exists": "false"
  },
  "then": {
```

```
    "effect": "deny"
  }
}
```

Best Practices:

- Define a standard tagging schema.

- Automate tagging during deployments using Bicep or ARM templates.

- Use Azure Policy to enforce and remediate tagging.

Data Governance and Compliance

Compliance is a legal and reputational requirement. Azure offers tools to automate and monitor regulatory compliance.

Recommendations:

- Enable **Azure Policy** to enforce configuration rules.

- Use **Compliance Manager** for tracking against standards like GDPR, ISO 27001, NIST.

- Apply **sensitivity labels** and **data loss prevention** (DLP) policies.

- Store audit logs for all critical services.

Azure Policy Example: Deny VMs without encryption enabled

```
{
  "if": {
    "not": {
      "field":
"Microsoft.Compute/virtualMachines/osDisk.encryptionSettings.enabled
",
      "equals": "true"
    }
  },
  "then": {
    "effect": "deny"
  }
}
```

Zero Trust Architecture

Adopt a **Zero Trust** model by assuming breach and verifying each request as though it originates from an open network.

Core Principles:

- **Verify explicitly** using strong authentication and authorization.

- **Use least privilege access** at every level.

- **Assume breach** and segment networks to minimize impact.

Zero Trust Tactics in Azure:

- Enforce Conditional Access and MFA.

- Use micro-segmentation with VNets and NSGs.

- Continuously monitor sessions and user behavior with Microsoft Defender.

Backup and Recovery

Even the most secure system can fail. A comprehensive backup strategy ensures resilience and business continuity.

Recommendations:

- Use **Azure Backup** for VMs, SQL databases, and file shares.

- Store backups in **different regions** for geo-redundancy.

- Regularly **test restore operations**.

- Enable **soft delete** and **immutability** for backup vaults.

Enable soft delete on Recovery Services vault:

```
az backup vault backup-properties set \
  --name myVault \
  --resource-group myRG \
  --soft-delete-feature-state Enabled
```

Summary

Securing a cloud deployment is a multifaceted and dynamic responsibility. By applying Azure best practices across identity, networking, storage, governance, and DevOps, organizations can significantly reduce their exposure to risk while maintaining agility and performance.

Key Takeaways:

- Always apply the **Principle of Least Privilege**.

- Implement **multi-layered security**, including network segmentation and encryption.

- Adopt **Zero Trust** and continuously verify all users and devices.

- Build security into the **DevOps lifecycle**.

- Enforce compliance using **Azure Policy**, **Blueprints**, and **Compliance Manager**.

- Monitor continuously using **Defender for Cloud**, **Azure Monitor**, and **Sentinel**.

- Plan for failure with **robust backup and recovery strategies**.

Security is not a set-it-and-forget-it discipline. As threats evolve, so too must your defenses. With proper governance, vigilant monitoring, and secure design principles, Azure provides the capabilities needed to deliver secure and trustworthy cloud solutions at scale.

Chapter 6: Cost Management and Optimization

Understanding Azure Pricing

Understanding Azure pricing is critical for organizations and individuals aiming to build scalable and sustainable cloud solutions. Without a clear grasp of how Azure services are priced, even the most technically sound solutions can result in unexpected expenses, budget overruns, and poor return on investment. This section explores the structure, components, and strategies involved in mastering Azure pricing.

The Basics of Azure Pricing

Azure pricing is based on a **pay-as-you-go** consumption model. Customers are billed based on their actual usage of services. This allows for significant flexibility but requires close monitoring to avoid waste.

Core characteristics of Azure pricing:

- **Per-minute or per-second billing** depending on the service

- **No upfront costs** (unless reserved instances are purchased)

- **Billing cycles** are monthly

- Services are priced regionally (i.e., same service may cost differently in different Azure regions)

Azure also supports other pricing models:

- **Reserved instances** (commitment for 1 or 3 years in exchange for discounts)

- **Spot pricing** (deep discounts for unused capacity, ideal for fault-tolerant workloads)

- **Hybrid Benefit** (bring your own license for Windows Server and SQL Server)

Azure Cost Structure Components

To understand pricing, it's important to break down the cost components by service type. Below is a high-level overview of how different services are typically billed:

Compute Services (e.g., Virtual Machines)

- **Per second** for running time (based on VM size)

- **OS type**, **region**, and **disk size** also affect pricing

- **Networking bandwidth** may incur separate charges

Example of VM pricing factors:

- VM type: `Standard_D2s_v3`

- Region: `UK South`

- Operating System: `Linux` or `Windows`

- OS Disk: `Premium SSD`, 128 GB

- Runtime: 720 hours/month

```
az vm list-sizes --location "uksouth"
```

Storage Services

- **Azure Blob Storage**: Charged per GB stored/month, per operation (read/write), and for data retrieval

- **Disk Storage**: Based on type (Standard HDD, Standard SSD, Premium SSD) and capacity

- **Azure Files**: Similar to Blob but optimized for SMB access

Additional factors:

- Redundancy (LRS, GRS, ZRS)

- Access tier (Hot, Cool, Archive)

Networking

- **Inbound data transfers**: Usually free

- **Outbound data transfers**: Charged per GB based on monthly volume

- **Public IP addresses**, VPN Gateways, ExpressRoute circuits, and Load Balancers may incur separate costs

Databases

- **Azure SQL Database**: Billed per DTU or vCore model

- **Cosmos DB**: Billed based on provisioned throughput (RU/s) and storage used

- **Storage, backups**, and **geo-replication** can influence total cost

App Services and Containers

- App Service Plans: Billed per instance, with tiers such as Free, Shared, Basic, Standard, Premium

- Azure Kubernetes Service (AKS): Control plane is free, VMs and other resources billed separately

- Azure Container Instances: Per-second billing for CPU and memory usage

Using the Azure Pricing Calculator

The Azure Pricing Calculator is a powerful tool for estimating costs before deployment. It allows you to configure and compare different service plans, regions, and options.

Steps:

1. Visit the Azure Pricing Calculator

2. Add services (e.g., Virtual Machine, SQL Database)

3. Configure region, tier, quantity, usage patterns

4. Review monthly cost breakdown

5. Export and share estimates as Excel or PDF

Tip: Always review pricing per **region** as there are cost differences even within the same service.

Understanding Azure Billing

Azure provides detailed billing and invoicing features via the **Cost Management + Billing** section in the Azure Portal.

Key terms:

- **Billing account**: Where the invoice is generated

- **Invoice section**: A sub-division of a billing account (for departments or teams)

- **Subscription**: A container for deployed services; usage is billed against this

Each subscription is associated with a billing account and can have different roles and access policies.

You can retrieve your current usage using Azure CLI:

```
az consumption usage list --start-date 2024-04-01 --end-date 2024-
04-30
```

Cost Analysis in Azure Portal

Cost Analysis is a visual tool that allows you to track and forecast your spending.

Benefits include:

- Cost breakdown by service, region, or resource group

- Trend analysis over time

- Budgets and alerts integration

- Filtering by tag or department

Steps to use Cost Analysis:

1. Go to Azure Portal → Cost Management + Billing

2. Select **Cost Analysis**

3. Choose **scope** (Subscription, Management Group, etc.)

4. Apply filters and groupings (e.g., Service name, Location, Tags)

Budgets and Alerts

To prevent overspending, you can define budgets that trigger alerts when costs exceed thresholds.

How to create a budget:

1. Azure Portal → Cost Management → Budgets

2. Create budget → Set name, amount, time period

3. Define alerts for percentages (e.g., 50%, 75%, 100%)

4. Add recipients (email, Action Groups)

Example: Budget of £1,000/month for dev subscription with email alert at 80%

```
az consumption budget create \
  --amount 1000 \
  --category cost \
  --name DevBudget \
  --start-date 2025-01-01 \
  --end-date 2025-12-31 \
  --time-grain monthly \
  --subscription <subscription-id> \
  --notifications \
    actual=80% \
    operator=GreaterThan \
    threshold=800 \
    contact-emails=user@example.com
```

Free Services and Cost-Free Options

Azure offers a number of **always-free services** and a **12-month free tier** for new customers.

Examples of always-free services:

-   750 hours/month B1S VM for 12 months

-   5 GB LRS Blob storage

-   250 GB SQL Database (Free Tier)

-   15 GB outbound data/month

Always explore the **free tier** when testing or developing small-scale projects.

Azure Hybrid Benefit and Reserved Instances

Two advanced cost-saving mechanisms:

- **Azure Hybrid Benefit**: Reuse your existing Windows Server and SQL Server licenses

- **Reserved Instances (RI)**: Save up to 72% by committing to 1-year or 3-year terms

Reserved Instance example via Azure CLI:

```
az vm reserved-vm purchase \
  --sku Standard_D2s_v3 \
  --term 1year \
  --billing-scope subscription \
  --region uksouth
```

Both options are ideal for workloads with predictable long-term usage.

Cost Tags and Governance

Use **tags** to track spending by project, environment, or department.

Example tag schema:

```
{
  "Environment": "Production",
  "Department": "IT",
  "Owner": "Frahaan",
  "CostCenter": "CC1001"
}
```

Use **Azure Policy** to enforce tagging:

```
{
  "if": {
    "not": {
      "field": "tags['Environment']",
      "exists": true
    }
  },
  "then": {
    "effect": "deny"
```

```
  }
}
```

Combine with **Management Groups** to group subscriptions for better financial control.

Forecasting Future Spend

Azure allows you to forecast costs based on current usage trends. Forecasts help you:

- Predict budget needs

- Adjust resources proactively

- Prevent sudden overages

To view forecasts:

1. Go to Azure Portal → Cost Management + Billing → Forecast

2. Select filters (subscriptions, time ranges)

3. Use filters and groupings for deeper insight

Summary

Azure's pricing structure is dynamic, flexible, and feature-rich—but it can become complex without proper knowledge and management. By understanding the core billing principles, using calculators and analysis tools, enforcing governance, and leveraging advanced pricing models, organizations can deploy cost-efficient solutions without surprises.

Key Takeaways:

- Azure bills on a pay-as-you-go model, with other options like reserved instances and spot pricing.

- Use the Azure Pricing Calculator and Cost Analysis for transparency and forecasting.

- Implement budgets, alerts, and tagging to enforce spending discipline.

- Optimize with Azure Hybrid Benefit, Reserved Instances, and region selection.

- Monitor costs proactively with Cost Management tools and CLI scripts.

- Always align cost decisions with business needs, workload criticality, and growth forecasts.

Mastering Azure pricing isn't just about avoiding unnecessary bills—It's about empowering teams to build smarter, faster, and more financially sustainable cloud solutions.

Tools for Budgeting and Forecasting

Budgeting and forecasting in Azure is essential for ensuring financial accountability, controlling costs, and planning future investments. Azure provides a robust set of native tools that help individuals, teams, and organizations track cloud spending, anticipate future costs, and align cloud investments with business goals.

In this section, we will explore Azure's budgeting and forecasting capabilities in depth, including how to use built-in tools such as Cost Management + Billing, Budgets, Forecasting, APIs, and automation strategies for financial governance. Understanding and utilizing these tools effectively is crucial for avoiding cost overruns and enabling predictable cloud expenditure.

Azure Cost Management + Billing

At the core of Azure's financial management offering is **Cost Management + Billing**, a unified service that provides access to all tools required for tracking, optimizing, and forecasting Azure spending.

From here, users can:

- View historical usage data

- Create and manage budgets

- Forecast future costs

- Analyze spending by resource, department, or tags

- Set up alerts and automated actions

To access:

1. Sign in to the Azure Portal.

2. Navigate to **Cost Management + Billing**.

3. Choose a **scope** (e.g., subscription, management group).

4. Explore **Cost Analysis**, **Budgets**, and **Forecast** tabs.

Azure Budgets

Azure Budgets allow you to set a financial threshold and track your actual and forecasted spending against that threshold. They are configurable at the subscription, resource group, or management group level.

Why use budgets?

- Detect cost overruns early.

- Notify stakeholders before thresholds are exceeded.

- Automate responses (e.g., shut down VMs or scale back services).

- Enforce financial discipline across teams and departments.

Creating a budget:

1. Go to **Cost Management + Billing → Budgets**.

2. Click **Add**.

3. Define the scope, budget amount, name, and duration.

4. Add **alerts** for threshold percentages (e.g., 80%, 90%, 100%).

5. Add **Action Groups** for notifications or automation.

Example using Azure CLI:

```
az consumption budget create \
  --amount 2000 \
  --category cost \
  --name ProductionBudget \
  --start-date 2025-01-01 \
  --end-date 2025-12-31 \
  --time-grain monthly \
  --subscription <your-subscription-id> \
  --notifications \
    actual=80% \
    operator=GreaterThan \
```

```
threshold=1600 \
contact-emails="finops@company.com"
```

Forecasting Future Costs

Azure provides built-in cost forecasting capabilities, allowing users to anticipate their spending based on historical trends. These forecasts can be used to plan budgets, reallocate funds, or scale resources appropriately.

Features of Azure Forecasting:

- Predictions based on actual usage and consumption trends.

- Visualization of expected costs in Cost Analysis.

- Options to forecast by **service**, **resource group**, **location**, or **tag**.

- Exportable reports for use in planning and review meetings.

How to view forecast:

1. Go to **Cost Management + Billing → Cost Analysis**.

2. Use the **Forecast** view from the chart type dropdown.

3. Apply filters to narrow the scope.

4. Review projected usage for the month or custom date ranges.

Forecasting example via REST API:

```
GET
https://management.azure.com/subscriptions/<subscriptionId>/provider
s/Microsoft.CostManagement/forecast?api-version=2023-03-01
Authorization: Bearer <token>
```

Cost Alerts and Automation

To respond proactively to budget thresholds and forecast deviations, Azure supports alerting and automation.

Budget alerts can be configured to:

- Send emails to stakeholders

- Trigger Azure Functions or Logic Apps

- Integrate with Microsoft Teams, Slack, or ITSM systems

- Enforce cost-saving actions (e.g., pause Dev/Test environments)

Example alert integration:

Use **Action Groups** to notify users:

```
az monitor action-group create \
  --name FinanceAlertGroup \
  --resource-group FinRG \
  --short-name FinAlert \
  --email-receivers name=FinanceTeam email=finance@company.com
```

Attach this group when creating a budget to ensure immediate notification.

Tagging for Budget Segmentation

Tagging resources is critical to breaking down budgets by department, project, or business unit. Tags allow for:

- Custom budget scopes

- Granular forecasting

- Departmental chargeback or showback

- Easier reporting and dashboarding

Best practices for tagging:

- Define a standard schema (e.g., Department, Project, CostCenter, Owner)

- Enforce tagging using Azure Policy

- Automate tag assignment with deployment scripts

Example tag policy to require CostCenter:

```
{
```

```
"if": {
  "not": {
    "field": "tags['CostCenter']",
    "exists": "true"
  }
},
"then": {
  "effect": "deny"
}
}
```

Apply this policy to ensure all resources contributing to a budget are properly categorized.

Scheduled Reports and Dashboards

Azure Cost Management supports exporting cost and usage data to:

- Power BI for advanced analytics

- Azure Storage for archival and integration with other systems

- Email-based reports for executives or department leads

To export cost data:

1. Go to Cost Management + Billing → Exports

2. Click + Add

3. Select scope, schedule (daily, weekly), and storage account

4. Configure file format (CSV) and delivery settings

This enables periodic reviews of spend and proactive forecasting.

Power BI Integration:

- Download the **Azure Cost Management connector** from Power BI Desktop

- Authenticate with Azure credentials

- Visualize spend by resource group, service, region, tag, and forecast

Programmatic Forecasting with APIs and SDKs

Advanced users can programmatically retrieve and analyze forecasting data using Azure SDKs and REST APIs.

Azure SDK for Python:

```python
from azure.identity import DefaultAzureCredential
from azure.mgmt.costmanagement import CostManagementClient

credential = DefaultAzureCredential()
client = CostManagementClient(credential)

scope = "/subscriptions/<subscription-id>"

forecast = client.forecast.usage(scope=scope)
print(forecast)
```

This enables integration with custom portals, reporting dashboards, or third-party tools.

Governance with Management Groups

Management groups allow you to manage budgets and forecasts at a higher level than individual subscriptions. This is particularly useful for enterprises managing multiple subscriptions across departments or business units.

Capabilities:

- Group subscriptions logically (e.g., by department, environment)

- Apply unified policies, budgets, and forecasts

- Aggregate cost data for high-level planning

Example hierarchy:

- Contoso Corp (management group)

  - Dev (subscription)

  - Test (subscription)

  - Prod (subscription)

You can apply a budget to the top-level management group to control aggregate spending.

FinOps Integration and Culture

Azure budgeting and forecasting tools work best when integrated into a broader FinOps (Financial Operations) strategy. FinOps promotes collaboration between finance, engineering, and product teams to make informed decisions about cloud usage.

Key cultural practices:

- Establish regular cost review meetings

- Empower teams with visibility into their own budgets

- Align cloud spend with business KPIs

- Treat forecast data as a planning tool, not just a report

Use Azure Cost Management data to drive conversations and decisions across departments, not just IT.

Summary

Budgeting and forecasting in Azure is not a one-time setup—it's a continuous process that requires strategy, visibility, and automation. By leveraging Azure's built-in tools and applying best practices, organizations can maintain financial control, reduce surprises, and make confident decisions about cloud investments.

Key Takeaways:

- Use **Azure Budgets** to define spending limits and trigger alerts.

- Leverage **forecasting tools** to anticipate usage and costs based on historical data.

- Tag resources consistently for precise budget segmentation and reporting.

- Automate alerts and responses using **Action Groups** and **Azure Functions**.

- Export and visualize cost data for business-level planning.

- Integrate budgeting into a **FinOps** culture to ensure cloud financial accountability.

With the right tools and approach, budgeting and forecasting become enablers of cloud innovation, not barriers to growth.

Tips to Avoid Unexpected Costs

Managing costs in Azure is not just about tracking usage—it's about proactively designing, configuring, and governing your resources to prevent unexpected charges. Cost overruns often occur due to resource sprawl, misconfigured services, underestimated workloads, or simply a lack of visibility into ongoing consumption.

This section provides comprehensive guidance on how to avoid unplanned expenses in Azure by implementing proven strategies, leveraging built-in tools, enforcing governance, and fostering a cost-conscious culture across teams.

Understand Your Baseline Usage

Before optimizing or limiting usage, it's essential to understand your **baseline consumption**. Without a baseline, it's nearly impossible to spot anomalies or track improvements.

Steps to establish a baseline:

1. Use **Cost Analysis** in Azure Portal to review the past 3–6 months of usage.

2. Group costs by **service**, **resource group**, **location**, and **tag**.

3. Identify consistently high-cost services or spikes.

4. Use **Exports** to analyze historical data externally in Excel or Power BI.

Export example via CLI:

```
az consumption usage list --start-date 2025-01-01 --end-date 2025-
01-31
```

Tracking and understanding your existing pattern sets the stage for responsible cost management.

Rightsize Resources

Overprovisioned services are a common cause of wasted spend. **Rightsizing** involves adjusting resource specifications to match actual demand.

Areas to focus on:

- **Virtual Machines**: Resize VMs based on CPU/memory utilization.

- **App Services**: Use the Basic or Standard tier unless Premium features are needed.

- **Databases**: Choose the right vCore/DTU levels, auto-pause where available.

- **Storage Accounts**: Use appropriate performance and redundancy tiers.

Use Azure Advisor to get recommendations for underutilized resources:

1. Go to Azure Advisor in the Portal.

2. Navigate to **Cost** recommendations.

3. Review suggestions like VM downscaling, shutting off unused disks, etc.

Resize VM example:

```
az vm resize --resource-group myRG --name myVM --size Standard_B2s
```

Use Auto-Shutdown and Auto-Scaling

Many resources—particularly dev/test environments—are left running outside business hours, incurring unnecessary charges.

Auto-Shutdown:

- Enable for VMs in non-production environments.

- Configure shutdown schedules using the Azure Portal or Automation.

Auto-Scaling:

- Scale App Services and Virtual Machine Scale Sets based on CPU usage or schedules.

- Prevent overprovisioning by dynamically adjusting capacity.

Enable VM auto-shutdown via CLI:

```
az vm auto-shutdown -g myRG -n devVM --time 1800 --email
admin@company.com
```

Configure auto-scale for App Service:

1. Azure Portal → App Service → Scale out

2. Add rule: Scale based on **CPU percentage**

3. Set thresholds, instance limits, and cooldown periods

Delete Unused or Orphaned Resources

Orphaned resources—such as unattached disks, unused IP addresses, or abandoned storage accounts—often go unnoticed but still generate costs.

Steps to identify unused resources:

- Use **Azure Advisor** for cleanup recommendations.

- Query resource inventory for unattached resources.

- Automate cleanup using Azure Automation or scripts.

Example: Identify unattached managed disks (PowerShell):

```
Get-AzDisk | Where-Object {$_.ManagedBy -eq $null}
```

Delete unused Public IPs (CLI):

```
az network public-ip delete --resource-group myRG --name myPublicIP
```

Implement Cost Alerts and Budgets

One of the most effective ways to avoid unexpected charges is by setting **budgets and cost alerts**.

Use cases:

- Notify when spend approaches 80%, 90%, or 100% of the budget.

- Trigger automation (e.g., stop VMs) when budgets are exceeded.

- Separate budgets by department, subscription, or project.

CLI Example:

```
az consumption budget create \
  --amount 1000 \
  --category cost \
  --name DevBudget \
  --time-grain monthly \
  --start-date 2025-01-01 \
  --end-date 2025-12-31 \
```

```
  --notifications actual=80% operator=GreaterThan threshold=800
contact-emails=admin@company.com
```

Use **Action Groups** for email, webhook, or function-based alerts.

Apply Tags for Cost Attribution

Proper tagging is essential for assigning costs to teams, environments, or applications.

Tag examples:

- `Environment: Production`

- `Department: Marketing`

- `Project: Alpha`

- `Owner: frahaan@company.com`

Tags allow:

- Filtering in Cost Analysis

- Applying policies and budgets at finer granularity

- Performing chargeback/showback processes

Apply tags using CLI:

```
az resource tag \
  --resource-id /subscriptions/<sub-
id>/resourceGroups/myRG/providers/Microsoft.Compute/virtualMachines/
myVM \
  --tags Department=Finance Environment=Test
```

Enforce tagging using **Azure Policy** to prevent resource creation without required metadata.

Choose the Right Pricing Tiers

Azure services often have multiple tiers, each with different capabilities and pricing. Choosing a higher tier than necessary can lead to inflated costs.

Examples:

- **App Services**: Don't choose Premium if Basic meets your needs.

- **Storage**: Use **Hot** tier for frequent access, **Cool/Archive** for infrequent access.

- **SQL Database**: Use **Serverless** or **Elastic Pools** for unpredictable or low-usage databases.

Understand the pricing model of each service and match it with actual workload requirements.

Switching storage tier (CLI):

```
az storage blob set-tier \
  --account-name mystorage \
  --container-name mycontainer \
  --name myblob \
  --tier Cool
```

Review and Optimize Networking Costs

Outbound data transfers, VPN gateways, NAT gateways, and load balancers can introduce significant costs.

Recommendations:

- Minimize outbound data (especially across regions or to the internet).

- Use **private endpoints** to avoid data egress charges.

- Monitor **ExpressRoute** and VPN costs.

- Use **Azure Firewall** logging to identify excessive outbound traffic.

Example: Estimate outbound data egress (CLI):

```
az monitor metrics list \
  --resource /subscriptions/<sub-
id>/resourceGroups/myRG/providers/Microsoft.Network/networkInterface
s/myNIC \
  --metric "BytesSent" \
  --interval PT1H
```

Understanding traffic patterns helps optimize routing and reduce unnecessary data movement.

Schedule Resource Deployment and Deletion

Use **automation scripts** or **Infrastructure as Code (IaC)** to deploy and tear down environments as needed.

- Great for training, proof-of-concept, or ephemeral workloads

- Automate using **Azure DevOps**, **GitHub Actions**, or **Terraform**

PowerShell example:

```
$deployTime = Get-Date
Remove-AzResourceGroup -Name "PoC-Env" -Force -Confirm:$false -
WhatIf
```

Terraform example:

```
resource "azurerm_resource_group" "example" {
  name      = "dev-env"
  location = "East US"
  lifecycle {
    prevent_destroy = false
  }
}
```

Destroy non-critical environments after hours to avoid idle cost accumulation.

Leverage Reserved Instances and Hybrid Benefits

If your workload is predictable, reserved instances (RI) can offer up to 72% cost savings.

RI Tips:

- Purchase for 1 or 3 years

- Scope to subscription or shared across billing accounts

- Can be exchanged or refunded

Enable Hybrid Benefit:

Bring existing licenses for Windows Server and SQL Server.

```
az vm update \
  --name myVM \
  --resource-group myRG \
  --license-type Windows_Server
```

This greatly reduces licensing costs, especially for long-running workloads.

Regular Cost Reviews and Optimization Sprints

Create a recurring process to review and optimize costs:

- Weekly cost email reports to stakeholders

- Monthly optimization sprint to review Azure Advisor and Cost Analysis

- Quarterly re-evaluation of resource sizing and architectural choices

Establish a **FinOps champion** in each department to promote ownership of cloud spend.

Summary

Avoiding unexpected costs in Azure requires a proactive and layered approach. By combining automation, monitoring, governance, and team accountability, you can prevent surprise bills and maximize the value of your cloud investments.

Key Takeaways:

- Establish usage baselines and monitor anomalies.

- Right-size compute, storage, and database resources.

- Schedule auto-shutdown and use scaling rules.

- Set budgets, cost alerts, and tagging policies.

- Remove unused resources and clean up regularly.

- Choose service tiers wisely and watch data egress.

- Leverage Reserved Instances and Azure Hybrid Benefit.

- Make cost optimization a regular part of your DevOps lifecycle.

With consistent attention and well-configured controls, your Azure environment can be both high-performing and cost-effective.

Scaling Up Without Overspending

Scaling in Azure is a powerful capability that allows organizations to dynamically adjust resources based on workload demand. However, without careful planning and management, scaling can lead to unnecessary cost increases, inefficient resource usage, and long-term financial waste. This section focuses on how to scale up applications, services, and environments in Azure intelligently—striking the right balance between performance, availability, and cost-efficiency.

Azure offers two primary scaling models: **vertical scaling** (increasing the capacity of a single resource) and **horizontal scaling** (adding more instances of a resource). Both must be handled with strategic oversight to avoid runaway costs.

Understand Your Workload Characteristics

Before scaling any system, it's essential to understand the nature of the workload:

- **Burst vs. steady**: Does the workload experience spikes or constant demand?

- **CPU-bound, memory-bound, or I/O-bound**: Which system component is the bottleneck?

- **Latency-sensitive vs. throughput-intensive**: What metric matters most?

Examples:

- A web API might scale horizontally during high traffic periods.

- A batch job may benefit from vertical scaling during scheduled processing.

- A reporting dashboard may remain idle most of the day but spike during business hours.

Using tools like **Azure Monitor**, **Application Insights**, and **Log Analytics**, you can collect metrics and logs to understand workload patterns.

Use Auto-Scaling Policies Intelligently

Auto-scaling adjusts the number of compute instances based on predefined rules. Azure supports auto-scaling for:

- **App Services**

- **Virtual Machine Scale Sets (VMSS)**

- **Azure Kubernetes Service (AKS)**

- **Azure Functions (with consumption plan)**

Configure smart scaling rules:

- Scale based on **CPU**, **memory**, or **custom metrics** (like queue length).

- Include **cool-down** periods to prevent flapping (frequent scale in/out).

- Set **minimum and maximum instance limits** to avoid budget overruns.

- Use **schedules** to scale predictably (e.g., more instances during business hours).

Example: Auto-scale rule for App Service:

1. Go to App Service → Scale out (App Service plan).

2. Add a rule: CPU > 70% for 5 minutes → increase instance count by 1.

3. Set scale-in rule: CPU < 30% for 10 minutes → decrease instance count by 1.

4. Set minimum: 1 instance, maximum: 5 instances.

Set up VMSS auto-scaling via CLI:

```
az monitor autoscale create \
  --resource-group myRG \
  --resource myVMSS \
  --resource-type Microsoft.Compute/virtualMachineScaleSets \
  --name autoscaleVMSS \
  --min-count 2 \
  --max-count 10 \
  --count 2

az monitor autoscale rule create \
```

```
--resource-group myRG \
--autoscale-name autoscaleVMSS \
--condition "Percentage CPU > 75 avg 5m" \
--scale out 1
```

Choose the Right Resource SKU

Selecting the optimal size (SKU) of resources is critical when scaling up. Overprovisioning a resource with more vCPUs or RAM than needed leads to waste, while underprovisioning results in performance issues.

Guidelines:

- Start small and increase incrementally.

- Monitor real-world usage with Azure Monitor.

- Use **Azure Advisor** to get SKU recommendations.

- Test performance using **Load Testing tools** before scaling up permanently.

VM SKU comparison (CLI):

```
az vm list-sizes --location uksouth --output table
```

Evaluate cost-performance ratios across SKUs to ensure you are getting value for money.

Optimize Scaling in App Services

Azure App Services supports multiple tiers (Free, Shared, Basic, Standard, Premium, Isolated). As you scale up, be sure you're selecting the right tier and instance count.

Tips:

- Use **Premium V2/V3** for production workloads that need higher IOPS and VNet integration.

- Evaluate **Isolated Tier** only for high-security or compliance requirements.

- Utilize **deployment slots** for zero-downtime deployments instead of additional apps.

Avoid cost traps:

- Don't overprovision instances.

- Use scaling rules instead of fixed instance counts.

- Consolidate apps onto fewer, higher-tier plans where possible.

Check App Service plan usage:

```
az appservice plan list --resource-group myRG --query
"[].{Name:name, Tier:sku.tier, Instances:sku.capacity}"
```

Utilize Serverless and Consumption-Based Models

Where appropriate, shift workloads to **serverless architectures** to scale automatically and pay only for actual usage.

Services to consider:

- **Azure Functions**: Scale based on event triggers.

- **Logic Apps**: Serverless workflows billed per action.

- **Azure Container Instances**: Lightweight container execution with per-second billing.

- **Event Grid, Service Bus**: Messaging systems that scale dynamically.

Azure Function sample billing strategy:

- First 1M requests and 400,000 GB-s free monthly

- After that: $0.20 per million executions

Serverless removes the need to pre-provision capacity, which helps minimize waste for variable or low-throughput workloads.

Use Scaling with Cost Constraints

Combine scaling mechanisms with **budgeting and alerts** to maintain financial control.

Steps:

1. Set up budgets on a per-resource group or subscription level.

2. Link **budget alerts** to scaling actions (e.g., scale in aggressively when cost hits 80%).

3. Apply **Azure Policy** to restrict resource sizes or prevent deployments in expensive regions.

Example: Azure Policy to restrict VM sizes:

```
{
  "if": {
    "field": "Microsoft.Compute/virtualMachines/sku.name",
    "notIn": ["Standard_B1s", "Standard_B2s", "Standard_D2s_v3"]
  },
  "then": {
    "effect": "deny"
  }
}
```

This helps ensure scaling decisions align with cost governance policies.

Design for Scale Efficiency

Architect your applications to be **scale-aware**. Scaling shouldn't be an afterthought—it should be a fundamental design decision.

Best Practices:

- Use **stateless architectures** to simplify horizontal scaling.

- Offload state to **Azure Storage**, **Redis**, or **Cosmos DB**.

- Design with **queue-based load leveling** to absorb traffic bursts.

- Use **caching** to reduce backend load (Azure Front Door, CDN, Redis).

- Defer non-critical workloads using **Durable Functions** or **Batch Jobs**.

These strategies reduce the pressure to scale up compute resources and can save significant costs.

Optimize Scaling for AKS and Containers

If you're using Azure Kubernetes Service (AKS) or containers, scaling involves additional layers like node pools, pods, and cluster autoscaling.

AKS Scaling Options:

- **Cluster autoscaler**: Adjusts node count based on pod demand.

- **Horizontal Pod Autoscaler (HPA)**: Scales pods based on CPU or custom metrics.

- **Vertical Pod Autoscaler (VPA)**: Adjusts pod resource limits automatically (still maturing in Azure).

Example: Enable cluster autoscaler (CLI):

```
az aks update \
  --resource-group myRG \
  --name myAKSCluster \
  --enable-cluster-autoscaler \
  --min-count 1 \
  --max-count 10
```

HPA configuration (YAML):

```
apiVersion: autoscaling/v2
kind: HorizontalPodAutoscaler
metadata:
  name: my-app
spec:
  scaleTargetRef:
    apiVersion: apps/v1
    kind: Deployment
    name: my-app
  minReplicas: 2
  maxReplicas: 10
  metrics:
  - type: Resource
    resource:
      name: cpu
      target:
        type: Utilization
        averageUtilization: 75
```

These features ensure that your containerized applications scale without overspending.

Monitor Scaling Impact in Real-Time

Scaling can have unintended consequences—both technically and financially. Continuous monitoring ensures you maintain balance.

Tools to use:

- **Azure Monitor**: Custom dashboards for scaling metrics.

- **Application Insights**: Detect performance issues from sudden scale-ins.

- **Log Analytics**: Query historical scaling events.

Sample KQL to track scale events:

```
AzureActivity
| where OperationNameValue contains "Scale"
| summarize Count = count() by ResourceGroup, ActivityStatusValue,
bin(TimeGenerated, 1h)
```

Review scale actions over time to refine your scaling strategies and policies.

Summary

Scaling in Azure offers tremendous power and flexibility, but must be executed with discipline to avoid overspending. Whether you're working with VMs, App Services, containers, or serverless architectures, the key is to balance performance needs with financial boundaries.

Key Takeaways:

- Understand workload patterns before scaling.

- Use auto-scaling rules with cooldowns and max limits.

- Choose the right SKUs and pricing tiers based on usage.

- Leverage serverless where appropriate to eliminate idle costs.

- Combine scaling with budgets, alerts, and policies.

- Architect applications to support scalable, cost-efficient patterns.

- Continuously monitor and adjust scaling strategies.

Scaling up doesn't have to mean scaling costs. With the right mix of planning, monitoring, and governance, Azure can provide both performance and cost-effectiveness at any scale.

Chapter 7: Troubleshooting and Support Essentials

Common Errors and How to Resolve Them

When working with Microsoft Azure, encountering issues is inevitable—whether it's during deployment, configuration, networking, or authentication. Developing a strong understanding of common problems and how to resolve them is critical for efficient cloud operations. This section dives deep into typical issues users face across different services and how to systematically troubleshoot and resolve them.

Understanding Azure's Error Messages

Azure services often generate error messages with codes and descriptions. These are your first clue in identifying what went wrong. The key components usually include:

- **Error Code** – A unique identifier like `InvalidTemplate`, `ResourceNotFound`, or `AuthorizationFailed`.

- **Message** – A more descriptive explanation of the issue.

- **Target** – Sometimes indicates which resource caused the problem.

Always take time to read and interpret the full message rather than skimming. It can save hours of troubleshooting.

Example:

```
{

  "error": {

    "code": "AuthorizationFailed",

    "message": "The client 'user@domain.com' with object id 'abc123'
does not have authorization to perform action
'Microsoft.Compute/virtualMachines/read' over scope
'/subscriptions/xxx/resourceGroups/myRG/providers/Microsoft.Compute/
virtualMachines/myVM'."

  }
```

```
}
```

Resolution: This means the user lacks permission to read a specific resource. Check Role-Based Access Control (RBAC) settings.

Troubleshooting Compute Issues

Virtual Machine (VM) Deployment Failures

Common Errors:

- `QuotaExceeded`: You've exceeded your regional limit for VM cores.

- `ImageNotFound`: The specified VM image doesn't exist.

- `InvalidTemplateDeployment`: Something's wrong in your deployment template.

Resolutions:

- Use the **Usage + quotas** section in the Azure portal to request quota increases.

- Validate the VM image URI via the Azure Marketplace or CLI.

- Use the following CLI command to test your deployment template:

```
az deployment group validate --resource-group myRG --template-file
azuredeploy.json
```

VM Startup Failures

Sometimes, a VM refuses to boot properly due to misconfigured OS, disk errors, or resource constraints.

Steps to Troubleshoot:

1. Use **Boot Diagnostics** in the VM blade to view the serial console or screenshot.

2. Detach the OS disk and attach it to a healthy VM for manual inspection.

3. Restore from snapshot or redeploy the VM if issues persist.

Troubleshooting Storage Issues

Blob Storage Access Denied

Common Error:

- `AuthenticationFailed` when trying to access a storage container.

Potential Causes:

- Using incorrect Shared Access Signature (SAS) token.
- Clock skew between client and Azure.
- Accessing with outdated storage keys.

Fixes:

- Regenerate SAS tokens.
- Sync system clock with a time server (use NTP).
- Regenerate access keys from the Azure portal if compromised.

Slow Performance on Azure Storage

Troubleshooting Approach:

- Check the replication tier: `LRS`, `GRS`, and `ZRS` impact latency.
- Use Azure Monitor to track metrics like `AverageE2ELatency`.
- Use correct blob tier: `Hot`, `Cool`, or `Archive` depending on usage.

Networking and Connectivity Issues

Inaccessible Web App or VM

Checklist:

- Is the Network Security Group (NSG) blocking the required port?

- Are the UDRs (User Defined Routes) configured correctly?

- Is the public IP bound to the right NIC?

Tools:

- **Network Watcher** → IP Flow Verify

- **Connection Troubleshoot** to check port accessibility

- Use PowerShell or CLI to test connectivity:

```
Test-NetConnection -ComputerName myvm.westus.cloudapp.azure.com -
Port 80
```

DNS Resolution Failures

Azure provides internal DNS services for VMs in virtual networks. If you're facing issues:

- Ensure `Azure-provided name resolution` is enabled in the VNet settings.

- Custom DNS may override internal resolution—double-check settings.

- Use `nslookup` or `dig` to debug DNS resolution from within a VM.

Authentication and Authorization Errors

Azure Active Directory Login Failures

Symptoms:

- Users can't sign into Azure Portal or CLI.

- Service Principals fail during deployments.

Steps to Resolve:

1. Validate that MFA (Multi-Factor Authentication) isn't blocking access.

2. Check Azure AD Sign-In logs.

3. Use `az login` for interactive login or `az ad sp create-for-rbac` for service principals.

```
az ad sp create-for-rbac --name myApp --role Contributor --scopes
/subscriptions/xxx
```

Role Assignment Delays

Even after assigning a role, it might take several minutes to take effect. In rare cases, it may not propagate properly.

Tips:

- Use the following CLI command to confirm role assignment:

```
az role assignment list --assignee user@domain.com
```

- If missing, try re-adding or waiting 5–10 minutes.

Troubleshooting ARM Template and Bicep Deployments

Deployments via Infrastructure-as-Code (IaC) can throw ambiguous errors.

Approach:

- Use `what-if` analysis to preview changes:

```
az deployment group what-if --resource-group myRG --template-file
main.bicep
```

- Always validate the schema with:

```
az bicep build --file main.bicep
```

- Modularize templates for clarity and easier debugging.

Monitoring and Diagnostic Logs

Effective troubleshooting often requires looking at logs.

Enable Logs:

- For VMs: Enable diagnostics settings for performance counters and boot logs.

- For Web Apps: Enable **Application Logging**, **Web Server Logging**, and **Detailed Error Messages**.

Log Access:

- Use **Log Analytics** to query logs.

- Example Kusto Query:

```
AppRequests

| where timestamp > ago(1h)

| where resultCode == "500"

| summarize count() by operation_Name
```

This identifies which operations are generating internal server errors.

Leveraging Azure CLI and PowerShell

Sometimes the Azure Portal doesn't expose enough details. CLI or PowerShell can offer deeper insight.

Examples:

List VM statuses:

```
az vm list -d -o table
```

Check resource provider registration:

```
az provider show --namespace Microsoft.Web
```

PowerShell Tip:

```
Get-AzVM -ResourceGroupName myRG -Status
```

Use automation scripts to detect and respond to known patterns.

Incident Management Best Practices

When an issue affects production systems:

1. **Document the Problem** – Start a log file with all observations.

2. **Classify Severity** – Determine business impact.

3. **Engage Stakeholders** – Notify impacted teams.

4. **Apply Fix** – Test in dev before pushing to prod.

5. **Post-Mortem** – After resolution, conduct a retrospective.

Escalation and Support

When you've exhausted all your options:

- Use **Azure Service Health** to check for platform outages.

- Open a support ticket from the Azure Portal.

- Choose the correct severity level based on business impact.

Before contacting Microsoft Support, prepare:

- Subscription ID

- Correlation ID (from failed request)

- Timestamp of error

- Diagnostic logs

Troubleshooting in Azure isn't just about fixing issues—it's about improving your architecture to prevent them. Invest time in root cause analysis, and use tools like Azure Advisor and Defender for proactive health checks.

Azure Support Plans and Resources

Managing support effectively in a cloud environment is just as important as architecting secure and scalable systems. Microsoft Azure offers multiple layers of support tailored to a wide range of user needs—from small development teams to enterprise-scale organizations. This section will explore in detail the various Azure support plans, how to engage with them, and what resources are available outside of paid support to empower teams to resolve issues faster and more independently.

Overview of Azure Support Tiers

Azure support is offered in several tiers, each designed for a different level of technical need and urgency. Understanding these tiers is essential for choosing the right level of coverage.

1. Basic Support (Free)

Included with all Azure subscriptions, the Basic plan provides access to:

- Azure documentation

- Community forums

- Status dashboards

- Limited billing and subscription support

This tier is suitable for individuals or teams learning Azure or using non-critical workloads.

2. Developer Support

- **Cost**: ~$29/month

- **Best for**: Non-production workloads and early-stage development

- **Response Time SLA**: <8 hours for "Minimal Impact" (Severity C) cases

Provides technical support during business hours and includes assistance with configuration, best practices, and general troubleshooting.

3. Standard Support

- **Cost**: ~$100/month

- **Best for**: Production workloads

- **Response Time SLA**:

  - <1 hour for critical cases (Severity A)

  - <4 hours for moderate impact (Severity B)

  - <8 hours for minimal impact (Severity C)

This tier includes 24/7 support for Severity A issues and is ideal for businesses hosting live systems on Azure.

4. Professional Direct (ProDirect)

- **Cost**: ~$1000/month

- **Best for**: Large teams with production-critical workloads

- **Features**:

  - Prioritized case handling

  - Proactive guidance from Azure advisors

- o   Operational reviews

- o   Webinars and tailored onboarding

5. Premier Support

- **Cost**: Custom pricing

- **Best for**: Enterprises with mission-critical workloads

- **Features**:

    - o   Dedicated account managers

    - o   Architecture reviews

    - o   Engineering-led support

    - o   Custom SLA agreements

Premier support is suitable for companies operating highly complex environments or requiring compliance support (e.g., financial or healthcare industries).

How to Create a Support Request

Support requests (tickets) can be created through the Azure Portal or via CLI.

Using the Azure Portal

1. Navigate to the **Help + support** blade.

2. Click on **Create a support request**.

3. Choose the issue type (technical, billing, subscription management, etc.).

4. Provide necessary details, including:

    - o   Problem description

    - o   Severity

    - o   Subscription ID

    - o   Affected service

    ○ Region

5. Submit the ticket.

You can track ticket status and responses in the **Support requests** section.

Using Azure CLI

```
az support ticket create --problem-class "technical" \

  --service-id "DZH315OXN0" \

  --title "VM not starting" \

  --description "My production VM is stuck in failed state." \

  --severity "critical"
```

Note: `--service-id` refers to the internal service mapping and should be retrieved beforehand.

Understanding Severity Levels

Azure uses severity levels to determine the priority of a support case.

Severity	Description	Typical Response Time (Standard Plan)
A	Critical impact: Production is down	<1 hour
B	Moderate impact: Degraded performance	<4 hours
C	Minimal impact: General questions/issues	<8 hours

You should only mark a ticket as Severity A if it affects live, production systems with no available workaround.

Self-Service Resources

Not every problem requires a support ticket. Azure has a wealth of resources to empower users to troubleshoot independently.

Azure Documentation

- https://docs.microsoft.com/azure

- Offers tutorials, how-to guides, and reference documentation for every service.

Microsoft Learn

An interactive learning platform offering role-based certification paths and sandbox environments.

Example learning path: **"Azure Fundamentals"**

```
https://learn.microsoft.com/en-us/training/paths/azure-fundamentals/
```

Azure Status Page

- URL: https://status.azure.com

- Displays current outages or service degradations across all regions.

- Useful to rule out platform-wide issues.

Azure Advisor

Azure Advisor is a free tool providing best practices and recommendations for:

- Cost optimization

- High availability

- Performance

- Security

It can preemptively detect configuration issues or inefficiencies that may eventually become support tickets.

Accessing Advisor

1. Go to the Azure Portal.

2. Search for **Advisor**.

3. Review recommendations per category.

Example recommendation:

```
"Your VM 'myVM' is underutilized. Consider resizing to a smaller SKU
to reduce cost."
```

You can export these recommendations and incorporate them into regular operational reviews.

Azure Service Health

While the status page shows broad outages, Azure Service Health gives personalized alerts related to your resources.

Features:

- Real-time outage notifications

- Planned maintenance updates

- Regional impact assessments

To configure alerts:

```
az monitor activity-log alert create \
  --name "ServiceHealthAlert" \
  --resource-group myRG \
```

```
--condition "level='Error'" \

--action-group
"/subscriptions/xxx/resourceGroups/myRG/providers/microsoft.insights
/actionGroups/myGroup"
```

Using Azure Diagnostics and Logs Before Opening Tickets

Microsoft expects that before you submit a technical support request, you've already gathered diagnostic data. This includes:

- **Activity Logs**

- **Resource Metrics**

- **Application Insights Data**

- **Azure Monitor Logs**

Gathering this data upfront helps Microsoft engineers resolve issues faster.

Example KQL query to retrieve failed deployments:

```
AzureActivity

| where operationNameValue ==
"Microsoft.Resources/deployments/write"

| where activityStatusValue == "Failed"

| project timeGenerated, resourceGroupName, properties
```

Best Practices for Engaging Support

1. **Be Detailed in the Problem Description**
   Provide steps to reproduce, the exact configuration, and what has already been attempted.

2. **Attach Logs and Screenshots**
   Upload screenshots of errors and JSON output from failed deployments.

3. **Keep Case Updated**
   Respond promptly when Microsoft requests more info to avoid ticket auto-closure.

4. **Use the Correct Language and Scope**
   Focus on symptoms and impact rather than assumptions about root cause.

Partner Support and Integration

Azure also offers a **Partner Support** channel for users working with Microsoft Partners. If your organization is working with a certified Microsoft Partner, they can raise and manage tickets on your behalf.

In some enterprise contracts, support is bundled and handled through the Partner, bypassing the need for you to manage tickets directly.

Escalating a Support Case

If you feel your issue isn't progressing:

- Use the **Escalate** button within the support request.

- Explain clearly why you are requesting escalation (e.g., no updates, delayed action, etc.).

- Escalation alerts a duty manager to reassign or prioritize your ticket.

Third-Party Communities and Tools

Sometimes peer-to-peer support can yield faster insights:

- **Microsoft Q&A**: https://learn.microsoft.com/answers

- **Stack Overflow**: Active Azure tag community.

- **Reddit**: Subreddits like r/AZURE can offer community-driven tips.

- **GitHub Issues**: For problems with SDKs and libraries.

Summary

Managing support effectively within Azure is more than simply reacting to issues—it involves choosing the right plan, knowing when and how to engage support, leveraging diagnostic data, and building operational awareness. Whether you're a solo developer or running a multi-region production system, Azure's layered support model ensures you can get help when needed—provided you know how to use it effectively. Investing in the right support tier and mastering self-service resources are strategic decisions that can significantly reduce downtime and enhance team productivity.

Logging and Diagnostics

Logging and diagnostics are fundamental to maintaining the health, performance, and security of applications and infrastructure on Microsoft Azure. In the cloud, where systems are often distributed and dynamic, traditional logging methods fall short. Azure provides a wide array of services, tools, and best practices to help organizations collect, analyze, and act upon logs and telemetry data effectively. This section explores in depth how to leverage Azure's built-in diagnostics and logging capabilities to support continuous monitoring, rapid troubleshooting, and operational excellence.

Why Logging and Diagnostics Matter

In modern cloud-based environments, logging serves several critical purposes:

- **Troubleshooting**: Helps pinpoint the source of errors, failures, and degraded performance.

- **Auditing**: Captures user actions and system events for security and compliance.

- **Monitoring**: Provides insight into application usage patterns, scalability, and reliability.

- **Automation**: Triggers alerts and responses through defined conditions.

- **Forecasting**: Enables predictive analysis for capacity planning and performance tuning.

Without robust logging and diagnostics, root cause analysis becomes time-consuming, and blind spots in infrastructure can lead to undetected failures.

Key Logging and Diagnostic Services in Azure

Azure offers multiple integrated services to handle logging and diagnostics across layers of the stack:

- **Azure Monitor**

- **Log Analytics**

- **Application Insights**

- **Azure Diagnostics Extension**

- **Activity Logs**

- **Azure Resource Logs**

- **Network Watcher Logs**

Each serves a specific role in the logging ecosystem.

Azure Monitor: The Core of Observability

Azure Monitor is a comprehensive platform for collecting, analyzing, and acting on telemetry from your Azure resources. It unifies data from:

- Applications (via Application Insights)

- Infrastructure (via Log Analytics)

- Custom sources (via Diagnostic settings)

Azure Monitor includes metrics and logs:

- **Metrics**: Lightweight, near real-time numerical values (e.g., CPU usage).

- **Logs**: Structured or unstructured data streams for deeper analysis.

You can route this telemetry to Log Analytics workspaces, storage accounts, or Event Hubs for further processing.

Application Insights: Deep Application-Level Telemetry

Application Insights is an APM (Application Performance Monitoring) service embedded in Azure Monitor. It collects detailed telemetry from applications including:

- Request rates, response times, and failure rates

- Dependency calls (SQL, HTTP, etc.)

- Exceptions and trace logs

- Custom events and metrics

- User and session analytics

Enabling Application Insights (ASP.NET Example)

```
public void ConfigureServices(IServiceCollection services)

{


services.AddApplicationInsightsTelemetry(Configuration["ApplicationI
nsights:InstrumentationKey"]);


}
```

Once enabled, data flows to the associated Application Insights resource where it can be queried using KQL (Kusto Query Language).

Log Analytics: Powerful Querying and Visualization

Log Analytics enables you to query large volumes of telemetry data stored in Azure Monitor. It supports structured queries through KQL and is ideal for:

- Root cause analysis

- Trend identification

- Security auditing

- Visual dashboards

Example: Find All Failed Requests

```
requests

| where resultCode == "500"

| summarize count() by cloud_RoleName, operation_Name
```

Example: High CPU VMs

```
Perf

| where ObjectName == "Processor" and CounterName == "% Processor
Time"

| summarize avg(CounterValue) by bin(TimeGenerated, 5m), Computer

| order by avg_CounterValue desc
```

Configuring Diagnostic Settings

Azure resources like VMs, storage accounts, and databases support **Diagnostic Settings** to control which logs and metrics are collected and where they are sent.

Supported Destinations:

- **Log Analytics workspace**

- **Storage Account (for long-term archiving)**

- **Event Hub (for integration with SIEM or external tools)**

Setting Up Diagnostics via Portal

1. Navigate to the resource (e.g., Virtual Machine).

2. Click on **Diagnostic settings**.

3. Select the logs and metrics to send.

4. Choose destination (Log Analytics, Storage, Event Hub).

5. Save the configuration.

Using CLI

```
az monitor diagnostic-settings create \

  --resource "/subscriptions/<sub-
id>/resourceGroups/myRG/providers/Microsoft.Compute/virtualMachines/
myVM" \

  --workspace "<log-analytics-id>" \

  --name "vmDiagnostics" \

  --logs '[{"category": "PerformanceCounters", "enabled": true}]'
```

Activity Logs vs Resource Logs

Activity Logs

- Capture **control plane** operations (e.g., create, delete, update resources).

- Useful for auditing administrative actions and API calls.

- Retained for 90 days by default.

Resource Logs

- Capture **data plane** operations inside Azure resources (e.g., disk reads/writes, database queries).

- Require explicit enabling through diagnostic settings.

Use both logs together for complete visibility.

VM Diagnostics Extension

Azure VMs require an agent to collect diagnostics like:

- CPU, memory, disk I/O metrics

- Application logs (Windows Event Logs, syslog)

- Boot diagnostics (screenshot and console output)

Installing the Extension (Linux example)

```
az vm diagnostics set \
  --resource-group myRG \
  --vm-name myVM \
  --settings ./diagnostic-config.json \
  --workspace "<workspace-id>"
```

Ensure the agent (Linux Diagnostic Extension or Windows Diagnostics Extension) is installed and configured properly.

Network Watcher and Network Logs

Azure Network Watcher offers tools to diagnose network-level issues.

- **NSG Flow Logs**: Show allowed/denied traffic through Network Security Groups.
- **Packet Capture**: Capture real-time traffic for in-depth analysis.
- **Connection Monitor**: Continuously checks the health of VM endpoints.

Enable Flow Logs

```
az network watcher flow-log configure \
  --resource-group myRG \
  --nsg myNSG \
  --enabled true \
  --retention 30 \
  --storage-account myStorage
```

Use these logs to investigate network latency, blocked ports, or unusual traffic patterns.

Diagnostics in Serverless and Container Environments

Azure Functions, Logic Apps, and Kubernetes (AKS) also support diagnostics.

Azure Functions

- Use **Application Insights** for logging.

- Log custom messages:

```
context.log("Function triggered with input:", input);
```

Azure Kubernetes Service (AKS)

- Integrate with **Container Insights**.

- Collect logs from stdout/stderr and Kubelet metrics.

- Use `kubectl logs` and `kubectl top` for on-the-spot diagnosis.

Logic Apps

- Enable diagnostics to export run history and trigger details.

- Useful when debugging integration workflows with connectors (e.g., SQL, Blob Storage, APIs).

Retention, Export, and Cost Management

Data Retention

- Logs stored in Log Analytics have configurable retention up to 2 years.

- Export logs to Azure Blob Storage for long-term archival if needed.

```
az monitor log-analytics workspace update \
```

```
  --resource-group myRG \

  --workspace-name myWorkspace \

  --retention-time 730
```

Cost Optimization

Logging can incur significant costs depending on volume and retention. To reduce cost:

- Use **sampling** in Application Insights.

- Filter unnecessary logs before ingestion.

- Use dedicated ingestion tiers for predictable billing.

Setting Up Alerts

Use Azure Monitor to set alerts based on logs and metrics.

Example: Alert for High CPU

```
az monitor metrics alert create \

  --name "HighCPU" \

  --resource-group myRG \

  --scopes
"/subscriptions/xxx/resourceGroups/myRG/providers/Microsoft.Compute/
virtualMachines/myVM" \

  --condition "avg Percentage CPU > 80" \

  --description "CPU usage is too high" \

  --action
"/subscriptions/xxx/resourceGroups/myRG/providers/microsoft.insights
/actionGroups/myActionGroup"
```

Alerts can notify you via email, SMS, webhook, or trigger automation runbooks.

Conclusion

Effective logging and diagnostics in Azure require more than enabling a few options—they demand a structured approach to telemetry collection, data analysis, and continuous feedback. By using tools like Azure Monitor, Application Insights, Log Analytics, and Network Watcher, teams can gain real-time and historical insights into their cloud infrastructure and applications. Investing in these practices improves system reliability, reduces time to resolution, and enables proactive performance tuning and security enforcement. Make diagnostics an integral part of every resource you deploy.

When to Reach Out to Microsoft Support

Despite thorough logging, diagnostics, and best practices, there are situations where you'll need to engage Microsoft Support directly. Knowing when and how to initiate this interaction can save time, minimize downtime, and ensure the appropriate urgency is applied. This section covers the scenarios that justify reaching out to Microsoft Support, the preparation needed beforehand, how to optimize communication during a support request, and how to follow up effectively. We'll also cover different channels of engagement and how to escalate unresolved issues.

Recognizing Support-Worthy Scenarios

Reaching out to Microsoft Support should not be your first step—it should be a strategic escalation after internal investigation. Below are scenarios where contacting support is not only appropriate but necessary:

1. Production Outages

When production workloads are down or severely degraded and impact revenue, service levels, or critical user operations:

- Virtual Machines refusing to start or boot

- Azure App Service is not responding

- Azure SQL or Cosmos DB unavailable or failing

- Authentication failures across services (e.g., Azure AD)

2. Platform Service Failures

Issues where Azure-managed services are not performing as expected despite configuration being correct:

- Azure Functions not triggering

- Logic Apps consistently failing

- Azure Kubernetes Service nodes failing to scale

3. Unexpected Billing or Cost Spikes

Large, unexplained increases in monthly charges should be investigated immediately:

- Unknown resource provisioning

- Misconfigured scaling leading to excessive consumption

- Overlapping or duplicated services

4. Security Breaches or Suspicions

Any indication of unauthorized access, compromised credentials, or tampered resources:

- Alerts from Microsoft Defender for Cloud

- Abnormal Activity Log entries

- Unexpected changes to configurations or RBAC roles

5. Service Quota Limitations

Encountering hard limits that block you from deploying or scaling:

- CPU, RAM, or VM Core limits per region

- Storage account limits

- Public IP address constraints

Support can assist in increasing quotas, typically after validation.

6. Global Azure Incidents

If a platform-wide service degradation impacts your services and no workaround is available, support can provide:

- Confirmation

- Temporary guidance

- Connection to the appropriate Microsoft teams

Always check https://status.azure.com and Azure Service Health before logging a ticket.

Preparing for Support Engagement

Efficient support depends on the quality of information provided. You should never open a case with a vague message like *"It's not working."* Instead, collect and present:

- **Summary of the issue**

- **Exact time the problem occurred**

- **Resource names and IDs**

- **Azure subscription ID**

- **Region and resource group**

- **Error messages or codes**

- **Logs and screenshots**

- **Steps to reproduce (if applicable)**

Example Support Ticket Summary

```
Summary: Azure Function not triggering on Event Grid event.


Environment: Production

Subscription ID: abc123-456def

Region: UK South

Resource: functionApp-prod-001


Observed Behavior:
```

- Event Grid is delivering events (confirmed via metrics)

- No function executions since 12:42 UTC

- No recent deployments or changes

- Function is healthy and shows "Ready" status

Steps Taken:

- Verified Event Grid Subscriptions

- Checked logs (no invocations)

- Restarted function app

This type of structured information speeds up case triage and avoids redundant questions from Microsoft engineers.

Opening a Support Ticket

There are multiple methods to open a support ticket. The most common is through the Azure Portal:

Portal Steps

1. Go to **Help + support** from the main menu.

2. Click **Create a support request**.

3. Choose **Issue Type**: Technical, Billing, Subscription Management, etc.

4. Select the **Service**, **Resource**, and **Problem Type**.

5. Enter **Issue Details**, **Severity**, and **Contact Info**.

6. Submit the request.

Azure CLI

```
az support ticket create \
```

```
--problem-class "technical" \

--title "SQL DB Timeout Errors" \

--description "SQL Database is intermittently returning timeout
errors starting from 10:15 UTC." \

--service-id "DZH3150XN0" \

--severity "moderate"
```

> Note: The `--service-id` needs to match the internal identifier for the affected Azure service.

Choosing Severity Levels Correctly

Microsoft Support triages tickets by severity, so you must choose appropriately:

Severity	Description	Typical Use Case
A – Critical	Production is down; urgent fix needed	App is completely offline, user access blocked
B – Moderate	Degraded performance; workaround exists	Function intermittently failing
C – Minimal	General questions or non-critical	Help with configuration or quota increase

Abusing Severity A will delay resolution and risk demotion if not justified. Only use it for actual production-impacting situations.

Working with Microsoft Engineers

Once your ticket is assigned, expect the following:

- Initial response time based on severity and support plan

- Request for additional diagnostic data

- Suggested troubleshooting steps

- Progress updates

Communication Best Practices

- Be responsive to emails or portal messages—delays on your end pause the SLA clock.

- Provide requested logs promptly.

- Keep discussions professional and focused on the technical problem.

You may be asked to perform actions such as:

- Enabling verbose logging

- Executing diagnostic scripts

- Sharing HAR files or network traces

- Granting temporary RBAC access to support personnel

Reopening and Following Up

If a ticket is closed but you feel the issue isn't resolved:

- Reopen the case from the portal within 14 days

- Add a detailed note explaining why you believe the issue persists

If you don't respond to a case update within a set period, Microsoft may auto-close the case. Be sure to set reminders or designate team members to follow up.

Escalation Path

If progress stalls or severity seems misjudged:

- Use the **Escalate** button in the support request view

- Clearly articulate the reason (e.g., "No update for 24 hours", "Incorrect diagnosis")

- Escalation brings in a duty manager to reassign or prioritize the case

  Note: Repeated, unjustified escalations can reduce future prioritization.

Leveraging Premier or ProDirect Support

For organizations with **Premier** or **ProDirect** support, additional pathways are available:

- **TAM (Technical Account Manager)**: Coordinate complex cases

- **Proactive Incident Reviews**: Identify root causes of past outages

- **FastTrack for Azure**: Design validation and architecture reviews

You can engage your account representative directly for priority routing of cases or if systemic issues emerge.

Third-Party and Indirect Support Paths

Some organizations work with:

- **Microsoft Partners**

- **Managed Service Providers (MSPs)**

These intermediaries can file support tickets on your behalf or offer additional escalation options. Always confirm your support arrangement in advance and clarify whether you're entitled to direct or partner-based support.

Support Analytics and Case History

From the **Help + support** blade, you can access the history of all support tickets:

- Filter by date, status, and severity

- Review resolution notes

- Export history for audits or internal KPIs

You can also use the **Azure Support API** to query ticket statuses programmatically.

After the Issue is Resolved

Once a case is resolved, follow these best practices:

1. **Perform a Post-Incident Review**
   Document what happened, what was done to resolve it, and how similar issues can be prevented.

2. **Update Internal Runbooks or SOPs**
   Integrate the solution into onboarding guides or runbooks to speed up future resolution.

3. **Automate Prevention**
   Use Azure Monitor alerts to detect the same pattern earlier in the future.

4. **Rate the Experience**
   Providing honest feedback helps Microsoft improve and supports stronger collaboration in future cases.

Summary

Microsoft Support is a vital component of Azure's operational model. Reaching out to support should be done with clarity, purpose, and preparation. Choose the right severity level, provide complete and actionable information, and maintain professional engagement throughout the lifecycle of the case. Whether you're using the Basic tier or Premier Support, your ability to interact effectively with Microsoft engineers can directly affect resolution time and service stability. Treat support as an extension of your DevOps or SRE team—not as a last resort—and build robust processes around it for sustained success in the cloud.

Chapter 8: Advancing Beyond the Basics

Intro to DevOps and Azure DevOps

DevOps is more than just a buzzword—it's a set of practices, tools, and cultural philosophies that bridge the gap between development and operations teams. By adopting DevOps, organizations can deliver applications and services faster and more reliably. Azure DevOps is Microsoft's comprehensive suite of services for implementing DevOps practices across the software development lifecycle (SDLC). In this section, we explore the foundations of DevOps, the services offered by Azure DevOps, real-world workflows, integration with other tools, and how to get started building a DevOps pipeline on Azure.

Understanding DevOps Philosophy

DevOps is built on the following core principles:

- **Collaboration** between development, operations, and quality assurance.

- **Automation** of repetitive tasks like testing, deployment, and configuration.

- **Continuous Integration and Continuous Deployment (CI/CD)** to ensure rapid, safe changes.

- **Monitoring and Feedback** loops for proactive problem resolution and improvements.

- **Infrastructure as Code (IaC)** to treat infrastructure the same way we treat application code.

These principles foster a high-trust environment that encourages frequent, smaller releases with quick rollback capability.

What is Azure DevOps?

Azure DevOps is a set of cloud-based tools that support the entire software delivery lifecycle. It includes:

- **Azure Repos**: Git repositories for source control.

- **Azure Pipelines**: Build and release pipelines for CI/CD.

- **Azure Boards**: Agile project tracking with Kanban boards and backlogs.

- **Azure Artifacts**: Package management for Maven, npm, NuGet, etc.

- **Azure Test Plans**: Manual and exploratory testing tools.

You can use the full suite or mix and match with external tools (e.g., GitHub, Jenkins, Jira).

Setting Up an Azure DevOps Organization

To begin using Azure DevOps:

1. Visit https://dev.azure.com

2. Sign in with your Microsoft account.

3. Create an **organization** (logical grouping for your DevOps work).

4. Inside the organization, create a **project** (for a specific application or workload).

Within the project, you gain access to:

- Boards for planning work

- Repos for storing code

- Pipelines for CI/CD

- Test Plans for QA

- Artifacts for dependency management

Azure Repos: Managing Source Code

Azure Repos provides private Git repositories that support:

- Branching strategies (e.g., GitFlow, trunk-based)

- Pull Requests with policy enforcement

- Code reviews and merge validations

Example Git Branch Policy:

- Require pull request reviews before merging

- Build validation (e.g., test suite must pass)

- Limit merges to certain users/groups

Azure Repos integrates tightly with Azure Pipelines for automation after commits or merges.

Azure Pipelines: CI/CD in Action

Azure Pipelines supports CI/CD for any language, platform, or cloud. It works with YAML or classic editor UI.

Example: Simple YAML Pipeline

```yaml
trigger:
  - main


pool:
  vmImage: 'ubuntu-latest'


steps:
  - task: UseNode@1
    inputs:
      version: '16.x'
  - script: npm install
  - script: npm test
    displayName: 'Run tests'
```

This pipeline triggers on commits to the main branch, installs dependencies, and runs tests.

Features of Azure Pipelines:

- Parallel jobs

- Self-hosted agents

- Environments and approvals

- Variable groups and templates

- Multi-stage pipelines

Azure Boards: Planning and Tracking Work

Azure Boards provides tools for Agile project management:

- **Work Items**: Tasks, bugs, epics, and user stories.

- **Backlogs and Sprints**: Organize and prioritize work.

- **Kanban Boards**: Visualize work-in-progress (WIP).

- **Dashboards**: Real-time status updates and metrics.

Boards integrate with Git commits, pull requests, and builds so you can link code to work items.

Example Workflow:

1. Create a user story → Assign it to sprint

2. Link commits and pull requests to the story

3. Monitor progress and burndown in dashboards

Azure Artifacts: Managing Packages

Azure Artifacts hosts private feeds for project dependencies:

- Supports npm, NuGet, Maven, Python, and Universal Packages

- Integrates with Azure Pipelines for publishing artifacts

- Controls who can publish or consume packages

Example: Publishing from Azure Pipeline

```
- task: DotNetCoreCLI@2

  inputs:

    command: 'pack'

    packagesToPack: '**/*.csproj'


- task: DotNetCoreCLI@2

  inputs:

    command: 'push'

    publishVstsFeed: '<feed-guid>'
```

Use Azure Artifacts to version and distribute internal libraries or tools securely.

Infrastructure as Code with Azure DevOps

One of the strongest benefits of DevOps is Infrastructure as Code (IaC), allowing reproducible environments.

Azure Pipelines can deploy:

- ARM Templates

- Bicep Files

- Terraform

- Ansible or other scripts

Example: Deploying ARM Template with Azure CLI

```
- task: AzureCLI@2

  inputs:

    azureSubscription: 'MyServiceConnection'

    scriptType: 'ps'

    scriptLocation: 'inlineScript'

    inlineScript: |

      az deployment group create \

        --resource-group myRG \

        --template-file azuredeploy.json
```

IaC ensures that every environment (dev, staging, prod) is consistent and trackable via source control.

Integrating External Tools

Azure DevOps can work alongside popular DevOps tools:

- **GitHub**: Use GitHub as the source repo, trigger Azure Pipelines on PRs or pushes.

- **Slack / Microsoft Teams**: Send build or deployment notifications.

- **Jenkins**: Trigger Jenkins jobs or import Jenkins artifacts.

- **ServiceNow**: Link incidents and change requests to pipelines.

Azure DevOps has a marketplace with 1000+ extensions to enhance capabilities or connect to 3rd-party platforms.

Testing and Quality Gates

Automation isn't just about deployment—testing is critical.

Azure Pipelines support:

- **Unit Tests** (e.g., NUnit, Mocha)

- **Integration Tests**

- **Code Coverage**

- **SonarCloud for Code Analysis**

- **Test Plans** for manual testing

You can define quality gates:

- Require >90% test pass rate

- Block releases with high code smells or vulnerabilities

- Stage rollouts with approval gates

Multi-Stage Release Pipelines

For complex deployments, use multi-stage pipelines to:

- Build once, deploy many times (Dev → QA → Prod)

- Add approvals, deployment conditions, and rollback logic

- Visualize pipeline execution as a flowchart

YAML Example:

```
stages:

  - stage: Build

    jobs:

      - job: BuildApp

        steps:

          - script: npm run build
```

```
- stage: Deploy

  dependsOn: Build

  jobs:

    - job: DeployApp

      steps:

        - script: az webapp deploy --name myApp
```

Each stage can target different environments, ensuring safe, progressive delivery.

Monitoring and Feedback in DevOps

Monitoring is not an afterthought in DevOps—it closes the loop.

Use:

- **Application Insights** for performance telemetry

- **Log Analytics** for infrastructure health

- **Azure Monitor Alerts** to trigger actions or escalations

- **Work Item Rules** to create bugs from failed pipelines

Example: Create an alert that opens a bug in Azure Boards when a pipeline fails 3+ times in a row.

```
- task: AzureDevOpsExtension@1

  inputs:

    connectedServiceName: 'myConnection'

    projectName: 'MyProject'

    workItemType: 'Bug'

    title: 'Investigate failing pipeline'

    description: 'Pipeline failed 3 consecutive times.'
```

Getting Started Tips

1. **Start Small**: Automate builds before jumping into full CI/CD.

2. **Use Templates**: Create reusable YAML templates to standardize practices.

3. **Version Everything**: Treat infrastructure, pipelines, and documentation as code.

4. **Secure Secrets**: Use Azure Key Vault or pipeline secrets for credentials.

5. **Iterate**: Improve pipeline complexity and resilience over time.

Summary

Azure DevOps empowers teams to build, test, deploy, and monitor applications efficiently through streamlined workflows and deep integration with Azure services. Whether you're building a microservices architecture or a monolithic app, using containers or serverless, DevOps practices—and Azure DevOps tools—can dramatically improve agility, quality, and collaboration. Embracing DevOps is not just about technology; it's a cultural shift toward automation, transparency, and continuous improvement. By starting with a single pipeline and expanding incrementally, any team can evolve into a high-performing DevOps organization.

Automating Deployments with ARM Templates

Automating infrastructure deployment is a cornerstone of modern cloud-native operations. Manual provisioning is slow, error-prone, and difficult to replicate across environments. Microsoft Azure provides several Infrastructure-as-Code (IaC) tools, with Azure Resource Manager (ARM) templates being the native and powerful choice for defining and deploying Azure resources in a declarative, repeatable way. This section explores ARM templates in detail, covering their structure, features, development, testing, deployment strategies, and integration into CI/CD pipelines. You'll also learn how to handle parameters, conditions, dependencies, modularization, and more.

What Are ARM Templates?

ARM templates are JSON files that define the infrastructure and configuration of Azure resources. They are executed by the Azure Resource Manager, which orchestrates resource provisioning in a declarative manner—meaning you define *what* you want, and Azure figures out *how* to make it happen.

Key properties:

- **Idempotent**: Deploying the same template multiple times produces the same result.

- **Declarative**: You define the desired state, not the steps to reach it.

- **Composable**: You can modularize and reuse components.

- **Parameterizable**: Supports input parameters for flexible deployments.

Basic Structure of an ARM Template

```json
{

  "$schema": "https://schema.management.azure.com/schemas/2019-04-01/deploymentTemplate.json#",

  "contentVersion": "1.0.0.0",

  "parameters": {},

  "variables": {},

  "functions": [],

  "resources": [],

  "outputs": {}

}
```

Sections Explained:

- **$schema**: Validates the structure and syntax.

- **contentVersion**: Version control for the template.

- **parameters**: Inputs for customization.

- **variables**: Constants or expressions to simplify reuse.

- **functions**: User-defined functions (optional).

- **resources**: Main section where you define infrastructure.

- **outputs**: Values returned after deployment (e.g., resource IDs).

Creating a Simple ARM Template

Example: Deploy a Storage Account

```
{

  "$schema": "https://schema.management.azure.com/schemas/2019-04-
01/deploymentTemplate.json#",

  "contentVersion": "1.0.0.0",

  "parameters": {

    "storageAccountName": {

      "type": "string",

      "metadata": {

        "description": "Name of the storage account"

      }

    }

  },

  "resources": [

    {

      "type": "Microsoft.Storage/storageAccounts",

      "apiVersion": "2022-05-01",

      "name": "[parameters('storageAccountName')]",

      "location": "[resourceGroup().location]",
```

```
    "sku": {

      "name": "Standard_LRS"

    },

    "kind": "StorageV2",

    "properties": {}

  }

 ]

}
```

This template takes a parameter for the storage account name and creates a `StorageV2` account with standard redundancy.

Parameters and Variables

Parameters

Parameters are used to pass dynamic values at deployment time. They can be simple types like strings and integers or complex objects.

```
"parameters": {

  "location": {

    "type": "string",

    "defaultValue": "eastus",

    "allowedValues": ["eastus", "westeurope"],

    "metadata": {

      "description": "Region to deploy the resources."

    }

  }

}
```

Variables

Variables store reusable expressions, improving maintainability.

```
"variables": {

  "storageSku": "Standard_LRS"

}
```

Using Outputs

Outputs are helpful for returning important values after deployment, such as resource IDs, connection strings, or hostnames.

```
"outputs": {

  "storageAccountId": {

    "type": "string",

    "value": "[resourceId('Microsoft.Storage/storageAccounts',
parameters('storageAccountName'))]"

  }

}
```

Deploying ARM Templates

You can deploy templates using the Azure Portal, CLI, PowerShell, or REST API.

Azure CLI

```
az deployment group create \

  --resource-group myResourceGroup \

  --template-file azuredeploy.json \
```

```
--parameters storageAccountName=mystorage123
```

PowerShell

```
New-AzResourceGroupDeployment `

  -ResourceGroupName "myResourceGroup" `

  -TemplateFile "azuredeploy.json" `

  -storageAccountName "mystorage123"
```

Conditional Logic and Loops

You can use condition and copy to control logic in ARM templates.

Condition

```
"condition": "[equals(parameters('createStorage'), 'yes')]"
```

Copy Loop

```
"copy": {

  "name": "storageLoop",

  "count": 3

}
```

This can be used to deploy multiple instances of the same resource type.

Handling Dependencies

Dependencies are automatically resolved by the ARM engine when a resource references another. However, you can explicitly declare them:

```
"dependsOn": [

  "[resourceId('Microsoft.Network/virtualNetworks', 'myVnet')]"

]
```

This ensures the VNet is created before a subnet or NIC.

Modularizing ARM Templates with Linked Templates

For complex deployments, split large templates into smaller, reusable linked templates.

Main Template:

```
{

  "resources": [

    {

      "type": "Microsoft.Resources/deployments",

      "apiVersion": "2021-04-01",

      "name": "linkedStorage",

      "properties": {

        "mode": "Incremental",

        "templateLink": {

          "uri":
"https://mystorage.blob.core.windows.net/templates/storage.json",

          "contentVersion": "1.0.0.0"

        },

        "parameters": {

          "storageAccountName": {

            "value": "[parameters('storageAccountName')]"
```

```
          }

        }

      }

    }

  ]

}
```

Testing ARM Templates

Before deploying, validate templates to catch errors:

CLI Validation

```
az deployment group validate \

  --resource-group myResourceGroup \

  --template-file azuredeploy.json
```

What-If Analysis

Preview the changes a template will make:

```
az deployment group what-if \

  --resource-group myResourceGroup \

  --template-file azuredeploy.json
```

This is a powerful feature that reduces risk during deployments.

Error Handling and Troubleshooting

ARM template deployments may fail due to:

- Incorrect resource names or types

- Quota limits

- Policy violations

- Missing dependencies

Tips:

- Use `Deployment Details` in Azure Portal to inspect each step

- Review error messages and correlate with documentation

- Use Activity Logs for insights into failed operations

Integrating ARM Templates in CI/CD

ARM templates can be deployed as part of Azure Pipelines or GitHub Actions.

Azure Pipelines Example

```
trigger:
  - main

jobs:
  - job: DeployInfra
    pool:
      vmImage: 'ubuntu-latest'
    steps:
      - task: AzureResourceManagerTemplateDeployment@3
        inputs:
          deploymentScope: 'Resource Group'
          azureResourceManagerConnection: 'MyServiceConnection'
```

```
subscriptionId: 'xxxx-xxxx-xxxx'

action: 'Create Or Update Resource Group'

resourceGroupName: 'myRG'

location: 'eastus'

templateLocation: 'Linked artifact'

csmFile: 'azuredeploy.json'

overrideParameters: '-storageAccountName mystorage123'
```

You can automate infrastructure delivery, validate changes, and manage deployments across environments.

Best Practices for ARM Templates

1. **Use Parameters Wisely**: Avoid hardcoding values—make templates reusable.

2. **Validate Early and Often**: Use validate and what-if before actual deployments.

3. **Modularize for Maintainability**: Separate large templates into linked templates.

4. **Use Naming Conventions**: Apply consistent and descriptive resource names.

5. **Source Control Everything**: Treat templates like code with versioning and code reviews.

6. **Use Secure Defaults**: Avoid public IPs, enable diagnostics, use role-based access controls.

7. **Document Templates**: Use metadata fields to describe parameters and outputs.

Transitioning from ARM to Bicep

Bicep is a domain-specific language (DSL) for ARM templates. It simplifies syntax while compiling down to ARM JSON.

Example Bicep vs ARM

Bicep:

```
resource storage 'Microsoft.Storage/storageAccounts@2022-05-01' = {

  name: 'mystorage123'

  location: resourceGroup().location

  sku: {

    name: 'Standard_LRS'

  }

  kind: 'StorageV2'

}
```

ARM JSON equivalent is more verbose. Bicep improves readability, supports modularization, and integrates with VS Code.

You can convert existing ARM templates to Bicep using:

```
az bicep decompile --file azuredeploy.json
```

Summary

ARM templates are an essential tool for automating the deployment of infrastructure in Azure. They offer precision, repeatability, and integration into CI/CD pipelines. While the learning curve can be steep due to the JSON syntax, the benefits in terms of control, governance, and speed are immense. By mastering ARM templates—and later Bicep—you enable your team to deploy environments confidently, reduce manual errors, and pave the way for fully automated, infrastructure-as-code-driven workflows. Adopt ARM templates today and build a more reliable, scalable Azure deployment strategy.

Exploring AI and Machine Learning in Azure

Artificial Intelligence (AI) and Machine Learning (ML) are reshaping how businesses operate, innovate, and make decisions. Azure provides a wide array of AI and ML services to help developers, data scientists, and enterprises build intelligent applications with minimal overhead. Whether you're developing sophisticated predictive models or adding prebuilt AI capabilities to your applications, Azure offers scalable, enterprise-grade tools to streamline the process. This section explores the rich ecosystem of Azure AI and ML services, their use cases, core components, deployment workflows, and real-world integration patterns.

Azure AI and ML: The Platform Overview

Azure provides multiple services under the AI and ML umbrella, including:

- **Azure Machine Learning (Azure ML)** – A full-featured platform for building, training, and deploying ML models.

- **Azure Cognitive Services** – Pretrained AI models accessible via simple APIs.

- **Azure OpenAI Service** – Access to powerful large language models like GPT-4.

- **Azure Synapse Analytics** – Integrated analytics platform with ML integration.

- **Azure Databricks** – Collaborative data science platform based on Apache Spark.

These services can be used individually or integrated into a pipeline depending on your use case, team structure, and technical needs.

Azure Cognitive Services

Cognitive Services provide ready-made AI models via REST APIs. They eliminate the need for building models from scratch and are ideal for rapid prototyping and production use.

Categories:

- **Vision**: Analyze images, extract text, recognize objects.

- **Speech**: Convert text to speech and vice versa, speaker recognition.

- **Language**: Text analytics, sentiment analysis, summarization.

- **Decision**: Personalization, content moderation.

- **Search**: Bing search APIs, autosuggestions.

Example: Analyzing Sentiment

```
curl -X POST
https://<region>.api.cognitive.microsoft.com/text/analytics/v3.0/sen
timent \
```

```
-H "Ocp-Apim-Subscription-Key: <your-key>" \

-H "Content-Type: application/json" \

-d '{

  "documents": [

    {

      "language": "en",

      "id": "1",

      "text": "Azure makes machine learning incredibly
accessible!"

    }

  ]

}'
```

The API will return a sentiment score and classification (positive, neutral, negative).

Azure OpenAI Service

Azure's OpenAI offering provides access to powerful foundation models like GPT-3.5, GPT-4, Codex, and DALL·E via REST and SDKs, backed by Azure's enterprise-grade security and compliance.

Use Cases:

- Chatbots

- Text summarization

- Code generation

- Semantic search

- Natural language interface to data

Example: Prompting GPT-4

```
{

  "messages": [

    {"role": "system", "content": "You are a helpful assistant."},

    {"role": "user", "content": "Summarize the article on Azure ML
for me."}

  ],

  "max_tokens": 100,

  "temperature": 0.7

}
```

Submit this to the `/chat/completions` endpoint to get a natural language summary.

Azure Machine Learning (Azure ML)

Azure Machine Learning is a cloud platform for managing the end-to-end ML lifecycle:

- **Data preparation**

- **Model training**

- **Model deployment**

- **Experiment tracking**

- **MLOps and versioning**

It supports no-code, low-code (Designer), and full-code experiences (SDK, CLI, Jupyter).

Key Components of Azure ML

1. **Workspaces** – Central management hub for ML assets.

2. **Datasets** – Versioned data storage and access.

3. **Compute Targets** – CPU/GPU clusters for training.

4. **Experiments** – Groups of related training runs.

5. **Pipelines** – Orchestrate end-to-end ML workflows.

6. **Models** – Registered, versioned models.

7. **Endpoints** – REST APIs for real-time or batch inference.

Training Models on Azure ML

Using Python SDK

```python
from azureml.core import Workspace, Experiment, ScriptRunConfig


ws = Workspace.from_config()
exp = Experiment(workspace=ws, name="my-experiment")


config = ScriptRunConfig(source_directory='./src',
                         script='train.py',
                         compute_target='cpu-cluster')


run = exp.submit(config)
run.wait_for_completion(show_output=True)
```

You can track metrics, download artifacts, and compare runs directly in the Azure portal or SDK.

Automated Machine Learning (AutoML)

Azure AutoML enables non-experts to generate models using best-practice techniques automatically.

- Supports classification, regression, time-series forecasting.

- Selects algorithms and tunes hyperparameters.

- Outputs interpretable models with performance metrics.

AutoML via Studio:

1. Upload dataset.

2. Choose target column and prediction type.

3. Configure compute.

4. Click *Start*.

Alternatively, use the Python SDK to automate the pipeline programmatically.

Deploying Models with Azure ML

You can deploy trained models as REST endpoints in two modes:

- **Real-time endpoints** (low-latency inference)

- **Batch endpoints** (scheduled or triggered bulk processing)

Example: Real-Time Deployment

```
from azureml.core.model import InferenceConfig

from azureml.core.webservice import AciWebservice


inference_config = InferenceConfig(entry_script='score.py',
environment=my_env)

deployment_config = AciWebservice.deploy_configuration(cpu_cores=1,
memory_gb=1)
```

```
service = Model.deploy(workspace=ws,

                       name='my-model-api',

                       models=[model],

                       inference_config=inference_config,

                       deployment_config=deployment_config)
```

Once deployed, your model is accessible via REST endpoint secured with keys or tokens.

Integrating ML with Applications

Models can be consumed from:

- Web APIs (e.g., Flask apps)

- Azure Functions

- Power Apps via custom connectors

- Logic Apps for workflows

- Azure Data Factory for batch inference

You can also embed predictions directly into reports using Power BI with Azure ML integration.

Monitoring and MLOps

Azure provides tools to operationalize ML:

- **Model monitoring**: Track data drift, accuracy degradation.

- **Version control**: Models, code, and pipelines can be versioned.

- **CI/CD**: Use Azure DevOps or GitHub Actions for ML deployment pipelines.

- **Model registry**: Manage and promote models through staging environments.

Azure ML supports integration with MLflow, enabling model tracking and lineage across environments.

Cost Considerations and Optimization

AI and ML workloads can be resource-intensive. Optimize usage by:

- Using **spot instances** for training

- Running jobs in **off-peak regions**

- Choosing **inference over training endpoints** for light models

- Automatically scaling compute clusters with `min_nodes` and `max_nodes`

Always monitor metrics like CPU, GPU usage, and job duration to avoid waste.

Real-World Scenarios

1. **Retail Forecasting**: Time-series models predict product demand using Azure ML.

2. **Call Center Intelligence**: Cognitive Services transcribe calls, analyze sentiment.

3. **Document Processing**: Form Recognizer extracts key data from invoices and receipts.

4. **Financial Risk Modeling**: Custom models predict loan default risk.

5. **Healthcare Diagnostics**: Images analyzed by trained CNNs deployed via real-time endpoints.

Getting Started Recommendations

- **Start with Cognitive Services** if you need fast AI without deep ML expertise.

- **Move to Azure ML** when building custom, domain-specific models.

- **Use the Studio UI** for initial exploration, then graduate to SDK for full automation.

- **Implement MLOps early** to ensure traceability, security, and scalability.

Resources to begin:

- Azure ML Studio: https://ml.azure.com

- Azure OpenAI: Available by application on [Azure Portal]

- Azure Cognitive Services Quickstarts: [https://learn.microsoft.com/en-us/azure/cognitive-services/]

Summary

Azure's AI and Machine Learning platform offers a versatile set of tools to meet a wide range of intelligent application needs. From fully managed, prebuilt APIs to advanced model training and deployment pipelines, Azure supports innovation across industries and skill levels. By leveraging Azure ML, Cognitive Services, and OpenAI, teams can build smarter solutions faster, maintain operational excellence, and drive competitive advantage. Mastery of these tools empowers you to transform data into actionable insights and build the future of intelligent software.

Certifications and Next Learning Paths

As cloud technologies continue to evolve rapidly, keeping your skills current is essential to remain competitive in the IT industry. Microsoft Azure certifications provide structured, recognized pathways to mastering Azure and validating your expertise. Whether you're an aspiring developer, a cloud architect, or a data professional, Azure's certification portfolio has a path for you. This section will guide you through the Microsoft certification ecosystem, detail the learning resources available, outline strategies for exam success, and help you plan your next steps after achieving certification.

Why Azure Certifications Matter

Azure certifications offer significant advantages for individuals and organizations alike:

- **Career Advancement**: Certified professionals are often prioritized in hiring and promotions.

- **Industry Recognition**: Certifications are globally recognized and respected across industries.

- **Practical Skills Validation**: They prove your hands-on expertise in real-world scenarios.

- **Learning Discipline**: Certification paths provide structured and goal-oriented learning.

- **Access to Resources**: Some certifications unlock additional training tools and partner benefits.

As of today, Microsoft certifications are mapped to job roles, making them highly relevant to your career goals.

Overview of Microsoft Azure Certification Levels

Microsoft certifications are organized into three main levels:

1. Fundamentals (Beginner)

Designed for individuals new to cloud concepts or Azure:

- **AZ-900: Microsoft Azure Fundamentals**

- **AI-900: Azure AI Fundamentals**

- **DP-900: Azure Data Fundamentals**

- **SC-900: Security, Compliance, and Identity Fundamentals**

These exams focus on basic concepts and require no prior experience.

2. Associate (Intermediate)

Ideal for professionals with some experience who want to deepen their skills:

- **AZ-104: Azure Administrator Associate**

- **AZ-204: Azure Developer Associate**

- **AI-102: Azure AI Engineer Associate**

- **DP-100: Azure Data Scientist Associate**

- **DP-300: Azure Database Administrator Associate**

- **SC-200: Security Operations Analyst Associate**

Associate-level certifications often serve as prerequisites for advanced specializations.

3. Expert (Advanced)

For professionals with deep experience designing or managing Azure solutions:

- **AZ-305: Azure Solutions Architect Expert**

- **SC-100: Microsoft Cybersecurity Architect**

- **DevOps Engineer Expert (AZ-400)** – Requires AZ-104 or AZ-204 as prerequisites.

Each exam has a unique code and corresponds to a specific role, helping you target your learning.

Deep Dive: Key Certifications

AZ-900: Microsoft Azure Fundamentals

This is the most accessible entry point for learning Azure. It covers:

- Cloud computing principles

- Core Azure services

- Security and governance

- Pricing and support

It's ideal for students, non-technical professionals, or anyone seeking a solid Azure overview.

AZ-104: Azure Administrator Associate

AZ-104 certifies your ability to manage Azure resources and includes:

- Azure subscriptions and governance

- Identity (Azure AD)

- Virtual networks

- Compute (VMs, App Services)

- Storage and backup

- Monitoring

Hands-on experience is highly recommended before attempting this exam.

AZ-204: Azure Developer Associate

Focuses on developing and deploying cloud applications:

- Azure SDKs and APIs

- App Service, Functions, Logic Apps

- Azure Storage and Cosmos DB

- Authentication and secure development

- CI/CD with Azure DevOps

Knowledge of C#, JavaScript/TypeScript, or Python will help.

AZ-305: Azure Solutions Architect Expert

Designed for senior architects who translate business needs into cloud solutions:

- Design compute, storage, networking, and security architectures

- Cost optimization and governance

- Business continuity and disaster recovery

- High availability and scalability

It is an advanced certification that requires deep understanding and prior experience.

Learning Resources and Tools

Microsoft provides official, free, and paid resources for exam preparation.

Microsoft Learn

- Self-paced, interactive modules

- Aligned directly to certification paths

- Free and updated regularly

Example: https://learn.microsoft.com/en-us/training/paths/azure-fundamentals/

Instructor-Led Training

Offered by Microsoft partners and training companies:

- Led by certified trainers (MCTs)

- Includes labs, real-time Q&A

- Can be expensive, but good for fast-tracking learning

Practice Exams

Third-party providers like MeasureUp and Whizlabs offer practice tests that simulate the real exam experience.

Labs and Sandboxes

- Microsoft Learn Sandbox: Free temporary environments

- Azure Free Tier: $200 credit for the first 30 days

- Visual Studio Dev Essentials: Access to free Azure hours and other tools

Use these to practice hands-on exercises, deployments, and real scenarios.

Strategies for Exam Success

1. **Understand the Exam Outline**

Each exam page lists skills measured. Use this as your study guide. Example for AZ-104:

- Manage Azure identities and governance (15–20%)

- Implement and manage storage (10–15%)

- Deploy and manage Azure compute resources (25–30%)

2. **Focus on Hands-On Practice**

Reading alone isn't enough. Deploy VMs, configure VNETs, use Azure CLI and PowerShell, set up App Services, and manage identity through Azure AD.

3. **Use the STAR Technique**

In questions with scenario-based formats, apply the STAR (Situation, Task, Action, Result) method to analyze choices.

4. **Join Study Groups**

Communities on LinkedIn, Reddit, or Tech Community offer accountability, motivation, and insights.

5. **Schedule the Exam in Advance**

Setting a date motivates consistent study. Microsoft offers exam scheduling via Pearson VUE or online proctored formats.

Cost and Retake Policy

- Most exams cost around **$99–$165 USD**

- Fundamental exams are often discounted or free via Microsoft events

- Retakes: If you fail, you can retake after 24 hours, but multiple failures require longer waiting periods

Also explore **Exam Replay Bundles**, which include retakes at a discounted rate.

Beyond Certifications: Continuous Learning Paths

Certifications are milestones, not endpoints. After certification:

1. Specialize Further

- Learn Bicep, Terraform, or Pulumi for Infrastructure as Code

- Explore Azure Synapse, Databricks, and ML pipelines

- Investigate service mesh, containers, AKS, and microservices

2. Advance to Multi-Cloud Skills

- Combine Azure expertise with AWS or GCP

- Use tools like HashiCorp Terraform that support multiple platforms

- Learn cloud-agnostic CI/CD with GitHub Actions, ArgoCD, or Jenkins

3. Contribute to the Community

- Share tips and experiences via blog posts or YouTube

- Join Microsoft Tech Community or local Azure Meetups

- Become a Microsoft Certified Trainer (MCT)

4. Pursue Microsoft MVP Status

The Microsoft MVP (Most Valuable Professional) program recognizes community leaders and evangelists. Contributions like content creation, public speaking, and open-source projects are considered.

Certification Maintenance and Updates

Certifications are valid for **1 year**. You can renew by completing a **free online assessment** on Microsoft Learn—no need to retake the full exam.

You'll receive reminder emails 6 months before expiration.

Keep an eye on changes to certification content. Microsoft often updates exams to reflect new Azure features, UI changes, or best practices.

Summary

Microsoft Azure certifications are a powerful way to validate your skills, enhance your career, and stay aligned with industry trends. From foundational knowledge in AZ-900 to advanced architecture in AZ-305, each certification unlocks new opportunities and areas of expertise. With a wide array of learning paths, tools, and communities available, there has never been a better time to invest in Azure certifications. Take your time, build real-world experience, engage with the ecosystem, and continue your journey into the ever-expanding world of cloud technology.

Chapter 9: Appendices

Glossary of Terms

The world of cloud computing, and particularly Microsoft Azure, comes with its own lexicon. Understanding the terminology is essential for effectively navigating the platform, configuring services, managing resources, and communicating with teams and stakeholders. This glossary provides detailed explanations of key terms, acronyms, and phrases that appear throughout this book and are frequently encountered when working with Azure.

Access Control List (ACL)
 A list that defines permissions attached to an object, such as a file or folder. In Azure, ACLs are often used with Azure Data Lake Storage and Azure Files to provide granular access control to data.

Active Directory (AD)
 A directory service developed by Microsoft for Windows domain networks. Azure Active Directory (Azure AD) is the cloud-based version used to manage identities and access in Azure environments.

ARM (Azure Resource Manager)
 The deployment and management service for Azure. It provides a management layer that enables you to create, update, and delete resources using templates, tools, and APIs.

Availability Set
 A logical grouping of VMs that allows Azure to understand how your application is built to provide for redundancy and availability. Helps ensure that VMs are spread across multiple fault domains and update domains.

Azure CLI
 A cross-platform command-line tool used to manage Azure resources. Useful for automating scripts and managing services without using the Azure portal.

```
# Example: Creating a resource group using Azure CLI

az group create --name MyResourceGroup --location eastus
```

Azure Functions
 A serverless compute service that allows you to run event-driven code without explicitly provisioning or managing infrastructure. Useful for automating small tasks, integrating services, and reacting to changes in data.

Blob Storage
 A storage service in Azure that is optimized for storing massive amounts of unstructured data like images, videos, backups, and logs.

Content Delivery Network (CDN)
A globally distributed network of servers that delivers content to users based on their geographic location. Azure CDN improves performance and reduces load on origin servers.

Cosmos DB
A globally distributed, multi-model NoSQL database service. Offers low latency, high availability, and elastic scalability.

Deployment Slot
A feature in Azure App Services that allows you to deploy different versions of your app in separate environments (slots), such as staging and production. You can swap between slots with minimal downtime.

DevOps
A set of practices that combine software development and IT operations. Azure DevOps provides developer services for support in planning work, collaborating on code development, and building and deploying applications.

Elasticity
The ability of a system to dynamically acquire or release resources to match demand. Azure services can automatically scale up or down based on usage patterns.

Endpoint
The URL or IP address used to connect to a cloud service or resource. Each Azure service exposes one or more endpoints to facilitate communication.

Firewall Rules
Configuration settings that define allowed IP ranges to access services like Azure SQL Database or Azure Storage Accounts. An essential security feature to prevent unauthorized access.

Geo-Replication
A feature that replicates data across multiple regions to ensure high availability and disaster recovery. Premium services like Azure Storage and Cosmos DB support this feature.

Hybrid Cloud
A computing environment that combines on-premises infrastructure with cloud services. Azure Arc extends Azure management and services to any infrastructure.

Identity and Access Management (IAM)
The practice of managing user identities and their permissions. Azure AD provides identity services, while RBAC (Role-Based Access Control) enables fine-grained access control.

Infrastructure as a Service (IaaS)
A cloud service model that provides virtualized computing resources over the internet. Azure Virtual Machines are a prime example of IaaS.

JSON (JavaScript Object Notation)
A lightweight data-interchange format often used in ARM templates and other Azure-related configurations.

```
{

  "type": "Microsoft.Storage/storageAccounts",

  "apiVersion": "2022-05-01",

  "name": "mystorageacct",

  "location": "eastus",

  "properties": {

    "accessTier": "Hot"

  }

}
```

Kubernetes (AKS - Azure Kubernetes Service)
An open-source platform for managing containerized workloads and services. AKS is Microsoft's managed Kubernetes offering for deploying and scaling containers.

Load Balancer
A networking service that distributes incoming traffic across multiple servers or instances to ensure high availability and reliability.

Logic App
A service for automating workflows and integrating apps, data, services, and systems using connectors and a visual designer.

Managed Identity
An identity in Azure AD that is automatically managed by Azure and used for authentication to services without storing credentials in code.

Multi-Factor Authentication (MFA)
A security system that requires more than one method of authentication to verify a user's identity. Typically combines a password with a device or biometrics.

Network Security Group (NSG)
A set of security rules that control inbound and outbound traffic to network interfaces, VMs, and subnets in an Azure virtual network.

PaaS (Platform as a Service)
A cloud service model that provides a platform allowing customers to develop, run, and manage applications without managing the underlying infrastructure. Azure App Services is an example.

Public IP Address
An IP address assigned to an Azure resource, making it accessible from the internet.

Quota
A preset limit on the resources that can be consumed. Examples include VM cores, storage limits, and subscription limits.

RBAC (Role-Based Access Control)
A method of regulating access to computer or network resources based on the roles of individual users within an organization. Azure RBAC is critical for secure resource management.

Region
A set of data centers deployed within a specific geographic location. Azure services are offered in multiple regions around the world.

Resource Group
A container that holds related resources for an Azure solution. It helps manage and organize resources collectively.

SaaS (Software as a Service)
A cloud service model in which software is provided over the internet as a service. Examples include Microsoft 365 and Salesforce.

Scalability
The ability of a system to handle increased load by adding resources. Azure services like App Service and Azure SQL Database can scale horizontally or vertically.

Service Principal
An identity created for use with applications, hosted services, and automated tools to access Azure resources. Often used in DevOps pipelines and automation scripts.

Storage Account
An Azure resource that provides access to storage services such as blobs, files, queues, and tables.

Subscription
An Azure subscription defines the set of resources that you can provision and use. It is linked to billing and access control.

Tags
Key-value pairs applied to Azure resources for categorization, billing, and management purposes.

Tenant
A dedicated instance of Azure AD that an organization receives when they sign up for Microsoft cloud services. It contains users, groups, and applications.

Throughput
The amount of data transferred or processed in a given period. Important for performance tuning of services like Cosmos DB and Azure SQL.

Virtual Machine (VM)
An IaaS offering that provides a virtualized server environment. You can configure OS, storage, and networking settings as needed.

Virtual Network (VNet)
The fundamental building block for private networking in Azure. VNets enable secure communication between resources, data centers, and the internet.

Web App
A feature of Azure App Services that enables hosting web applications in a fully managed environment.

Zone Redundancy
A high availability offering that replicates data and resources across multiple availability zones within a region to protect from datacenter failures.

This glossary is by no means exhaustive, but it serves as a foundational reference. As you deepen your journey with Azure, continue to explore official documentation, community forums, and certifications to expand your cloud vocabulary and proficiency.

Resources for Further Learning

As the cloud landscape evolves rapidly, continuous learning is essential for maintaining technical proficiency and staying current with best practices. This section provides a comprehensive collection of resources—spanning official documentation, hands-on labs, training platforms, books, communities, podcasts, newsletters, and certification support. Whether you are just beginning your Azure journey or looking to specialize in a specific domain, the following tools and platforms will support your long-term growth and mastery of Microsoft Azure.

Microsoft Learn

https://learn.microsoft.com

Microsoft Learn is the official platform for free, interactive, self-paced training. It offers structured learning paths, modules, sandboxes, quizzes, and certifications. Features include:

- **Role-based learning paths** (e.g., Azure Administrator, Developer, Security Engineer)

- **Certification-aligned content** (e.g., AZ-104, AZ-900, AZ-204)

- **Integrated sandbox environments** for hands-on labs with no Azure subscription required

- **Progress tracking** tied to your Microsoft account

Recommended learning paths:

- *Azure Fundamentals* – Great for beginners

- *Develop and Deploy Apps on Azure* – For application developers

- *Architecting Microsoft Azure Solutions* – For solution architects

---

Official Microsoft Documentation

https://learn.microsoft.com/en-us/azure

The official Azure documentation portal contains:

- Service-specific docs (e.g., Azure Functions, Cosmos DB, AKS)

- Quickstarts and tutorials

- REST API references

- Architectural best practices

- Feature announcements and updates

Use the documentation to understand syntax, constraints, pricing, service limits, and integration options.

Azure Architecture Center

https://learn.microsoft.com/en-us/azure/architecture/

This is a must-read for solution architects and developers designing complex workloads. It features:

- **Reference architectures**

- **Design principles**

- **Best practices**

- **Industry blueprints** for regulated industries like finance and healthcare

- **Scalability and security guidance**

Use it as a reference when designing enterprise-grade, secure, and cost-efficient cloud systems.

Microsoft Cloud Adoption Framework

https://learn.microsoft.com/en-us/azure/cloud-adoption-framework/

The Cloud Adoption Framework helps enterprises strategize and manage the transition to cloud technologies. It includes:

- Strategy planning guides

- Governance and compliance models

- Migration tools and playbooks

- Organizational alignment and change management

Ideal for IT leaders, project managers, and consultants involved in digital transformation efforts.

Microsoft Azure Blog

https://azure.microsoft.com/en-us/blog/

The Azure Blog is a rich source of product announcements, deep-dives, roadmap previews, and customer stories. Categories include:

- Compute

- Data

- Security

- DevOps

- Industry Solutions

Subscribe to stay up to date with new features and architectural trends.

GitHub Repositories

GitHub is a valuable hub for real-world samples, SDKs, and open-source Azure tools.

Key repositories to follow:

- https://github.com/Azure/azure-quickstart-templates: 1,000+ deployment examples using ARM and Bicep templates.

- https://github.com/Azure-Samples: Language and service-specific code samples.

- https://github.com/MicrosoftDocs: Community-editable versions of Microsoft documentation.

Use GitHub to clone examples, learn implementation patterns, and contribute to the community.

Community Forums and Discussion Boards

Microsoft Q&A

https://learn.microsoft.com/en-us/answers/topics/azure.html

A moderated forum where Azure users and Microsoft engineers answer technical questions.

Stack Overflow

https://stackoverflow.com/questions/tagged/azure

Ideal for quick help with specific development or configuration issues. Use tags like `azure-functions`, `azure-devops`, `azure-cli`, etc.

Reddit

- **r/AZURE**: A large community discussing Azure deployments, pricing, challenges, and tips.

These communities can provide quick answers, experience-based guidance, and real-world insights.

Books and eBooks

For deeper and more structured learning, consider these recommended titles:

- *Exam Ref AZ-900 Microsoft Azure Fundamentals* by Jim Cheshire

- *Exam Ref AZ-104 Microsoft Azure Administrator* by Harshul Patel

- *Microsoft Azure Architect Technologies and Design* by Brett Hargreaves

- *Azure for Architects* by Ritesh Modi

- *The Azure Cloud Native Architecture Mapbook* by Stephane Eyskens

Many are available via Packt, Microsoft Press, or O'Reilly.

Video Courses and Certifications

Pluralsight

https://www.pluralsight.com/paths/microsoft-azure

- Courses aligned with Microsoft exams

- Hands-on labs and assessments

- Skill IQ for tracking learning progress

LinkedIn Learning

https://www.linkedin.com/learning/

- Professional courses in Azure, DevOps, and certification prep

- Taught by industry experts and MCTs

- Integrated with LinkedIn profiles

Coursera and edX

Offer Microsoft-created certification paths, including hands-on Azure projects and capstones.

Hands-On Labs and Sandboxes

Microsoft Learn Sandbox

Interactive, browser-based labs that give you temporary Azure subscriptions to complete learning modules. No setup required.

Azure Lab Services

https://learn.microsoft.com/en-us/azure/lab-services/

Used to create lab environments for classrooms, training events, or testing scenarios.

Newsletters and Podcasts

Azure Weekly

https://azureweekly.info/

Curated Azure news, blog posts, and updates delivered to your inbox.

Microsoft Source

https://techcommunity.microsoft.com

A feed of technical news, webinars, and community highlights.

Azure DevOps Podcast

Covers real-world implementation stories, CI/CD strategies, and Azure DevOps platform deep dives.

CloudSkills.fm

Discusses cloud certifications, career paths, and interviews with cloud professionals.

Azure CLI and PowerShell Learning Resources

Mastering automation tools like CLI and PowerShell is vital for real-world efficiency.

CLI Documentation

https://learn.microsoft.com/en-us/cli/azure/

Includes install guides, command references, and examples.

PowerShell for Azure

https://learn.microsoft.com/en-us/powershell/azure/

Covers installation, module references, and scripting examples.

Example CLI Script

```
az vm create \

  --resource-group myResourceGroup \

  --name myVM \

  --image UbuntuLTS \

  --admin-username azureuser \

  --generate-ssh-keys
```

Practice scripting daily tasks to reduce deployment time and improve reproducibility.

Azure Roadmaps and Change Logs

Azure Updates

https://azure.microsoft.com/en-us/updates/

Tracks newly released features and public previews.

Microsoft Build / Ignite Sessions

Rewatch keynotes, demos, and technical deep-dives from Microsoft's largest developer and IT conferences.

Getting the Most from These Resources

1. **Curate a Personal Learning Path**
   Combine Microsoft Learn with hands-on practice, certification books, and GitHub examples.

2. **Engage with the Community**
   Ask questions, share insights, and contribute to discussions on forums or GitHub.

3. **Stay Consistent**
   Set weekly goals—one module, one tutorial, or one lab—and track your progress.

4. **Build Real Projects**
   Apply what you learn in side projects. Create web apps, deploy APIs, automate with ARM templates.

5. **Document Your Journey**
   Blogging or posting on LinkedIn reinforces learning and helps others follow in your footsteps.

Summary

Learning Azure is an ongoing journey that rewards hands-on experience, curiosity, and community engagement. By combining official resources with community-driven platforms, practice labs, and structured certifications, you can continuously expand your cloud expertise. Azure's fast pace of innovation means there's always something new to learn—embrace it by making learning a daily habit, and you'll be well-equipped for any cloud challenge that comes your way.

Sample Projects and Code Snippets

Nothing accelerates learning and retention more effectively than building real-world projects. This section provides a series of curated sample projects and reusable code snippets designed to help you apply your Azure knowledge in meaningful ways. These projects span infrastructure automation, web app deployment, serverless computing, AI integration, and CI/CD pipelines. Each one includes a high-level overview, key implementation steps, and sample code to kickstart development. By working through these examples, you'll develop both confidence and capability in deploying, managing, and scaling solutions on Azure.

Project 1: Deploy a Static Website on Azure Storage

Objective: Host a simple HTML/CSS/JS website using Azure Blob Storage with static website hosting enabled.

Steps:

1. Create a storage account.

2. Enable static website hosting.

3. Upload website files via Azure Portal or CLI.

4. Access via the provided web endpoint.

Sample CLI Script:

```
az storage account create \

  --name mystaticweb \

  --resource-group myRG \

  --location eastus \

  --sku Standard_LRS


az storage blob service-properties update \

  --account-name mystaticweb \

  --static-website \

  --index-document index.html \

  --error-document 404.html


az storage blob upload-batch \

  --account-name mystaticweb \

  --source ./website \

  --destination '$web'
```

This is a perfect starter project to explore Azure's serverless web hosting capability.

Project 2: Deploy a Full-Stack Web App Using App Service and Azure SQL

Objective: Deploy a full-stack application (e.g., Flask, Node.js, or ASP.NET) connected to an Azure SQL Database.

Steps:

1. Create an App Service plan and web app.

2. Create an Azure SQL Database and configure firewall access.

3. Set connection strings as environment variables in App Service.

4. Deploy app via GitHub Actions or Azure CLI.

Sample Connection String:

```
Server=tcp:myserver.database.windows.net,1433;Initial Catalog=mydb;

Persist Security Info=False;User ID=myadmin;Password=myPassword123;

MultipleActiveResultSets=False;Encrypt=True;TrustServerCertificate=False;

Connection Timeout=30;
```

Add this as an App Setting named SQLCONNSTR_mydb in the Azure Portal.

GitHub Actions Deployment Snippet:

```yaml
- name: Deploy to Azure Web App

  uses: azure/webapps-deploy@v2

  with:

    app-name: 'mywebapp123'

    slot-name: 'production'

    publish-profile: ${{ secrets.AZURE_WEBAPP_PUBLISH_PROFILE }}

    package: '.'
```

Project 3: Build a Serverless Workflow with Azure Functions and Logic Apps

Objective: Process form submissions with Azure Functions and trigger notifications via Logic Apps.

Architecture:

- HTML form posts to an HTTP-triggered Azure Function.

- Function stores data in Cosmos DB.

- Logic App sends an email when a new entry is added.

Azure Function Code (JavaScript):

```javascript
module.exports = async function (context, req) {

    const data = req.body;

    context.bindings.outputDocument = JSON.stringify(data);

    context.res = {

        status: 200,

        body: "Submission received"

    };

};
```

Bindings in `function.json`:

```json
{

  "bindings": [

    {

      "authLevel": "function",

      "type": "httpTrigger",
```

```
    "direction": "in",

    "name": "req",

    "methods": ["post"]

  },

  {

    "type": "http",

    "direction": "out",

    "name": "res"

  },

  {

    "type": "cosmosDB",

    "name": "outputDocument",

    "direction": "out",

    "databaseName": "formDB",

    "collectionName": "submissions",

    "createIfNotExists": true,

    "connectionStringSetting": "CosmosDBConnection"

  }

 ]

}
```

Project 4: Deploy Infrastructure with Bicep Templates

Objective: Use Infrastructure as Code to deploy a virtual network and virtual machines.

Steps:

1. Install Bicep CLI.

2. Create a `.bicep` template defining a VNet, subnet, and VM.

3. Deploy using Azure CLI.

Sample Bicep Template:

```
param location string = resourceGroup().location

param vmName string


resource vnet 'Microsoft.Network/virtualNetworks@2021-05-01' = {

  name: 'myVNet'

  location: location

  properties: {

    addressSpace: {

      addressPrefixes: ['10.0.0.0/16']

    }

    subnets: [

      {

        name: 'default'

        properties: {

          addressPrefix: '10.0.1.0/24'

        }

      }

    ]

  }

}
```

```
resource vm 'Microsoft.Compute/virtualMachines@2021-07-01' = {

  name: vmName

  location: location

  properties: {

    hardwareProfile: {

      vmSize: 'Standard_B1s'

    }

    storageProfile: {

      imageReference: {

        publisher: 'Canonical'

        offer: 'UbuntuServer'

        sku: '18.04-LTS'

        version: 'latest'

      }

      osDisk: {

        createOption: 'FromImage'

      }

    }

    osProfile: {

      computerName: vmName

      adminUsername: 'azureuser'

      adminPassword: 'P@ssw0rd1234!'

    }
```

```
    networkProfile: {

      networkInterfaces: [

        {

          id: '/subscriptions/<sub-
id>/resourceGroups/myRG/providers/Microsoft.Network/networkInterface
s/nic1'

        }

      ]

    }

  }

}
```

Project 5: Setup CI/CD for a Node.js API with Azure DevOps

Objective: Build and deploy a Node.js backend API to Azure App Service using Azure DevOps.

Steps:

1. Create a new project in Azure DevOps.

2. Connect a Git repository.

3. Define a `azure-pipelines.yml` file for build and release.

4. Link your App Service in the deployment stage.

Sample `azure-pipelines.yml`:

```
trigger:

  - main
```

```yaml
pool:

  vmImage: 'ubuntu-latest'


steps:

  - task: NodeTool@0

    inputs:

      versionSpec: '16.x'

    displayName: 'Install Node.js'


  - script: npm install

    displayName: 'Install dependencies'


  - script: npm run build

    displayName: 'Build the project'


  - task: ArchiveFiles@2

    inputs:

      rootFolderOrFile: 'dist'

      includeRootFolder: false

      archiveType: 'zip'

      archiveFile: '$(Build.ArtifactStagingDirectory)/build.zip'


  - task: PublishBuildArtifacts@1

    inputs:
```

```
    PathtoPublish: '$(Build.ArtifactStagingDirectory)'

    ArtifactName: 'drop'


- task: AzureWebApp@1

  inputs:

    azureSubscription: '<Your-Service-Connection>'

    appName: '<your-app-name>'

    package: '$(System.ArtifactsDirectory)/drop/build.zip'
```

Project 6: Automate Resource Cleanup with Azure PowerShell

Objective: Automatically delete unused VMs or test environments after a defined retention period.

PowerShell Script:

```
Connect-AzAccount

$threshold = (Get-Date).AddDays(-7)

$vms = Get-AzVM | Where-Object { $_.Tags["expireOn"] -and (Get-Date
$_.Tags["expireOn"]) -lt $threshold }


foreach ($vm in $vms) {

    Remove-AzVM -ResourceGroupName $vm.ResourceGroupName -Name
$vm.Name -Force

    Write-Output "Deleted VM: $($vm.Name)"

}
```

Schedule this as an Azure Automation runbook to keep test environments tidy and reduce cost.

Project 7: Real-Time AI Sentiment Analysis Chatbot

Objective: Build a chatbot that receives user input, sends it to Azure Cognitive Services for sentiment analysis, and responds accordingly.

Architecture:

- Bot Framework SDK (Node.js)

- Azure Bot Service

- Azure Text Analytics API

Sample Bot Reply Logic:

```
const sentiment = await analyzeSentiment(userInput);

if (sentiment === 'negative') {

    await context.sendActivity("I'm sorry to hear that. Want to talk
about it?");

} else {

    await context.sendActivity("That's great! How can I assist you
further?");

}
```

This project combines real-time communication, AI, and serverless architecture.

Tips for Customizing Projects

- **Parameterize everything** for environment flexibility.

- Use **Secrets in Key Vault** instead of hardcoding credentials.

- Add **tags** to all deployed resources for traceability and cost analysis.

- Implement **logging and monitoring** via Azure Monitor, Application Insights, and Log Analytics.

- Use **Terraform** or **Pulumi** as alternatives to ARM/Bicep for a multi-cloud approach.

Summary

Hands-on projects are the most effective way to internalize Azure concepts. The examples in this section are designed to help you build functional solutions while exposing you to the full range of Azure services—from basic web hosting to advanced AI and infrastructure automation. As you work through these examples, try extending them with new features, automating deployment with pipelines, and integrating with external systems. These projects lay a solid foundation for portfolio development, interviews, certifications, and real-world success in cloud engineering.

API Reference Guide

This API reference guide serves as a comprehensive resource for developers and IT professionals interacting with Microsoft Azure programmatically. Azure offers multiple APIs that allow you to provision, manage, monitor, and automate cloud resources and services. This guide covers the primary APIs available, their use cases, authentication mechanisms, request structures, SDK integrations, and real-world usage patterns. Whether you're building custom dashboards, deploying infrastructure, or automating workflows, mastering Azure APIs is key to building scalable and efficient solutions.

Overview of Azure API Types

Azure provides several types of APIs, each suited for different use cases:

- **Azure REST API** – Direct, low-level interaction with Azure services over HTTPS.

- **Azure SDKs** – Language-specific libraries built on top of REST APIs.

- **Azure Resource Manager (ARM) API** – For deploying and managing resources.

- **Microsoft Graph API** – Unified API for accessing Microsoft 365 and Azure AD.

- **Azure Data Plane APIs** – For interacting with data within services (e.g., Blob Storage, Cosmos DB).

- **Azure CLI/PowerShell** – Command-line wrappers around APIs for scripting.

This guide focuses on REST APIs and SDK equivalents for key services.

Authentication with Azure APIs

Before calling any Azure API, you must authenticate using Azure Active Directory (Azure AD). There are two primary methods:

1. Client Credentials (App-Only)

Used for service-to-service interactions without user involvement.

- Register an app in Azure AD

- Generate a client secret or certificate

- Use it to obtain an access token from Azure AD

Token Request Example:

```
curl -X POST https://login.microsoftonline.com/<tenant-id>/oauth2/v2.0/token \

  -H "Content-Type: application/x-www-form-urlencoded" \

  -d "client_id=<client-id>&scope=https://management.azure.com/.default&client_secret=<client-secret>&grant_type=client_credentials"
```

2. Interactive Authentication (User Delegated)

Used for scenarios requiring a user's identity (e.g., portals, dashboards).

- Redirect user to login page

- Consent to requested scopes

- Use access token for API requests

Common API Request Format

Azure REST API requests typically follow this structure:

```
GET
https://management.azure.com/subscriptions/{subscriptionId}/resource
Groups/{resourceGroupName}/providers/Microsoft.Compute/virtualMachin
es?api-version=2023-03-01

Authorization: Bearer <access_token>

Content-Type: application/json
```

Components:

- **Base URL**: `https://management.azure.com`

- **Resource path**: Identifies what you're working with (VMs, databases, etc.)

- **Query string**: Always includes `api-version`

- **Headers**: Include `Authorization` and `Content-Type`

ARM API: Creating a Virtual Machine

Endpoint:

```
PUT
https://management.azure.com/subscriptions/{subscriptionId}/resource
Groups/{resourceGroupName}/providers/Microsoft.Compute/virtualMachin
es/{vmName}?api-version=2023-03-01
```

Request Body (Partial):

```
{
  "location": "eastus",
  "properties": {
    "hardwareProfile": {
      "vmSize": "Standard_B1s"
```

305 |

```
        },

        "storageProfile": {

          "imageReference": {

            "publisher": "Canonical",

            "offer": "UbuntuServer",

            "sku": "18.04-LTS",

            "version": "latest"

          }

        },

        "osProfile": {

          "computerName": "myvm",

          "adminUsername": "azureuser",

          "adminPassword": "Password123!"

        }

      }

    }

  }
```

Use this API to programmatically deploy infrastructure or integrate provisioning into internal systems.

Azure Storage API (Data Plane)

To upload, download, or manage blobs, use the Blob Storage REST API.

Upload a Blob:

```
PUT https://<account>.blob.core.windows.net/<container>/<blob>

Authorization: SharedKey <account>:<signature>
```

```
x-ms-blob-type: BlockBlob

x-ms-date: <date>

x-ms-version: 2021-12-02

Content-Length: <length>
```

Sample SDK Usage (Python):

```python
from azure.storage.blob import BlobClient


blob = BlobClient.from_connection_string(conn_str, container_name,
blob_name)

with open("file.txt", "rb") as data:

    blob.upload_blob(data)
```

Azure SQL API

Azure SQL Database is managed through the ARM API and T-SQL endpoints.

List Databases in a Server:

```
GET
https://management.azure.com/subscriptions/{subscriptionId}/resource
Groups/{resourceGroupName}/providers/Microsoft.Sql/servers/{serverNa
me}/databases?api-version=2021-11-01
```

You can manage performance tiers, firewall rules, auditing, and geo-replication using REST or Azure CLI.

Azure Cognitive Services API

Provides AI-as-a-Service via prebuilt models for vision, speech, and language.

Example: Sentiment Analysis API

```
POST
https://<region>.api.cognitive.microsoft.com/text/analytics/v3.2/sen
timent

Ocp-Apim-Subscription-Key: <your-key>

Content-Type: application/json
```

```
{

  "documents": [

    {

      "id": "1",

      "language": "en",

      "text": "Azure APIs are powerful and easy to use."

    }

  ]

}
```

The response includes sentiment scores and classifications.

Microsoft Graph API

Used to access Microsoft 365 services and Azure AD data.

Get User Profile:

```
GET https://graph.microsoft.com/v1.0/me

Authorization: Bearer <access_token>
```

List Azure AD Users:

```
GET https://graph.microsoft.com/v1.0/users

Authorization: Bearer <access_token>
```

Microsoft Graph is essential for identity, compliance, and user profile management scenarios.

Monitoring and Diagnostics API

You can query Azure Monitor metrics and logs via REST.

Get Metrics for a VM:

```
GET
https://management.azure.com/subscriptions/{subscriptionId}/resource
Groups/{resourceGroup}/providers/Microsoft.Compute/virtualMachines/{
vmName}/providers/microsoft.insights/metrics?api-version=2023-03-
01&metricnames=Percentage%20CPU

Authorization: Bearer <token>
```

You can integrate metrics into third-party dashboards or automation logic.

Azure DevOps REST API

Manage pipelines, repositories, builds, and more via the Azure DevOps REST API.

Trigger a Pipeline:

```
POST
https://dev.azure.com/{organization}/{project}/_apis/pipelines/{pipe
lineId}/runs?api-version=7.0-preview.1

Authorization: Basic <base64 PAT>
```

Get Pipeline Status:

```
GET
https://dev.azure.com/{organization}/{project}/_apis/build/builds/{b
uildId}?api-version=7.0
```

Use these APIs for CI/CD pipeline orchestration and monitoring.

Azure SDKs and Language Support

Azure offers SDKs in multiple languages:

- **.NET** – `Azure.ResourceManager`, `Azure.Storage.Blobs`, `Microsoft.Graph`

- **Python** – `azure-mgmt-resource`, `azure-storage-blob`, `azure-identity`

- **JavaScript/TypeScript** – `@azure/arm-resources`, `@azure/storage-blob`

- **Java** – `com.azure.resourcemanager`, `com.azure.identity`

- **Go** – `github.com/Azure/azure-sdk-for-go`

SDKs wrap REST APIs and handle authentication, retries, and pagination internally.

Automation Scenarios Using APIs

Provision Environments on Demand

Use REST APIs or SDKs to dynamically spin up environments for testing, development, or demos.

Centralized Billing Dashboards

Pull usage and cost data from APIs and build custom dashboards in Power BI or internal portals.

Governance and Compliance Audits

Use the Graph API to query user permissions, role assignments, and audit logs.

Auto Scaling Logic

Invoke REST APIs to scale VMs or App Services in response to custom metrics or alerts.

Best Practices

- **Use SDKs where possible**: They simplify authentication, retries, and error handling.

- **Secure credentials**: Store tokens and secrets in Azure Key Vault.

- **Handle pagination**: Many API responses include `nextLink` for large result sets.

- **Monitor rate limits**: Some services throttle high-volume API usage.

- **Enable logging**: Record all API interactions in mission-critical workflows for traceability.

Summary

The Azure API landscape is vast, enabling you to manage every aspect of your infrastructure and services programmatically. Whether interacting with the management layer through the ARM API, accessing identity data via Microsoft Graph, or deploying apps using Azure DevOps, APIs are foundational to automation and integration. Mastery of REST APIs, combined with effective use of SDKs and CLI tools, empowers you to create scalable, secure, and automated cloud solutions. Use this guide as a starting point and reference as you deepen your Azure development and operations expertise.

Frequently Asked Questions

In this final section of the book, we address the most commonly asked questions about Microsoft Azure—covering topics from setup and administration to architecture, automation, cost management, security, and certification. Whether you're new to Azure or a seasoned professional, these FAQs provide quick answers and practical guidance drawn from real-world experience and the most pressing community queries. Each question is followed by a concise explanation or step-by-step answer to help you take immediate action.

Getting Started

Q: Do I need a credit card to sign up for Azure?
A: Yes. A credit or debit card is required to verify your identity, even for the free tier. You will not be charged unless you explicitly upgrade to a paid subscription after your initial free usage or spending limit ends.

Q: What is included in the Azure free tier?
 A: The free tier includes 12 months of popular services (e.g., Virtual Machines, Blob Storage, SQL Database), 25+ services always free, and $200 of credits to explore any Azure service within the first 30 days.

Q: How do I choose between Azure CLI, PowerShell, and the Portal?
 A:

- Use **Azure CLI** for cross-platform scripting and automation.

- Use **Azure PowerShell** if you're deeply integrated into Microsoft ecosystems (Windows, Active Directory).

- Use the **Azure Portal** for visual navigation, quick tests, and resource inspection.

Resource Management

Q: What's the difference between a subscription, a tenant, and a resource group?
 A:

- A **tenant** represents a dedicated instance of Azure Active Directory.

- A **subscription** is tied to a billing account and used to organize resources.

- A **resource group** is a logical container within a subscription that holds related Azure resources.

Q: Can I move resources between regions?
 A: Not all resources support direct regional moves. Some, like VMs and Storage Accounts, must be re-created in the new region, and data migrated manually or via Azure Resource Mover.

Q: How can I tag my resources effectively?
 A: Use a standard naming convention with tags such as:

- Environment: Dev, Test, Prod

- Owner: User or Team Name

- CostCenter: Accounting code

- Project: Project name or ID

Tags help with cost management, automation, and compliance tracking.

Security and Identity

Q: What is the difference between Azure AD and Active Directory?
A:

- **Active Directory (AD)**: On-premises directory service for Windows domain networks.

- **Azure Active Directory (AAD)**: Cloud-based identity and access management for apps and services, supporting SSO, MFA, conditional access, and B2B/B2C scenarios.

Q: How can I enforce Multi-Factor Authentication (MFA)?
A: Use Conditional Access policies in Azure AD. Navigate to Azure AD > Security > Conditional Access > Create Policy, and configure MFA for specific users, apps, or sign-in conditions.

Q: What is a service principal?
A: A service principal is an identity created for an application or automation tool to access Azure resources securely using RBAC. It's commonly used in CI/CD pipelines or script automation.

Cost Management

Q: How do I avoid unexpected charges?
A:

- Set up **budgets and cost alerts** in Azure Cost Management.

- Use **resource tagging** for cost attribution.

- Leverage the **Azure Pricing Calculator** before deploying.

- Regularly review the **Cost Analysis** blade to identify trends and spikes.

Q: What are Reserved Instances?
A: Reserved Instances (RIs) allow you to save up to 72% on compute resources by committing to a one- or three-year term. They are best suited for predictable workloads like long-running VMs or SQL databases.

Q: Can I get notified when spending exceeds a threshold?
A: Yes. Create a budget in Cost Management with an alert threshold (e.g., 80% of $100). Azure will email the notification to designated users.

Networking and Performance

Q: How do I allow traffic to a VM from the internet?
A:

1. Assign a public IP to the VM.

2. Open required ports in the **Network Security Group (NSG)** attached to the VM or subnet.

3. Optionally configure DDoS protection or firewall rules.

Q: What's the difference between VNet and Subnet?
A:

- A **VNet** is an isolated virtual network in Azure.

- A **Subnet** is a segmented range within a VNet, used to organize and apply security policies to groups of resources.

Q: How do I enable private access to PaaS services like Azure Storage?
A: Use **Private Endpoints** to create a private IP connection from your VNet to Azure Storage, SQL, or other PaaS services. This prevents exposure to the public internet.

Automation and DevOps

Q: What's the difference between ARM templates and Bicep?
A:

- **ARM templates** use verbose JSON syntax for infrastructure as code.

- **Bicep** is a simplified, more readable DSL that compiles into ARM templates. Both are supported and deployable via Azure CLI and DevOps pipelines.

Q: Can I automate resource creation using GitHub Actions or Azure DevOps?
A: Absolutely. Use Azure CLI or PowerShell scripts within CI/CD workflows to deploy ARM/Bicep templates, applications, or updates.

Q: What is Azure Blueprints?
 A: Azure Blueprints help automate the deployment of compliant environments by packaging ARM templates, policies, role assignments, and resource groups into reusable artifacts.

Monitoring and Diagnostics

Q: How can I monitor the health of my Azure resources?
 A: Use **Azure Monitor** and **Log Analytics** to track performance, availability, and diagnostics. Enable **diagnostic settings** on each resource to send logs to a centralized Log Analytics workspace.

Q: What are Azure Alerts?
 A: Alerts notify you of critical conditions based on metric thresholds or log query results. They can trigger email notifications, webhooks, or automated runbooks.

Q: How can I get notified when my web app goes down?
 A:

1. Enable **Application Insights** on your App Service.

2. Create an **Availability Test**.

3. Set up an **alert rule** based on failed test count.

4. Connect it to an **Action Group** to receive alerts.

Storage and Databases

Q: What's the difference between Blob, File, Disk, and Queue Storage?
 A:

- **Blob**: Object storage for unstructured data.

- **File**: Managed file shares (SMB/NFS) in the cloud.

- **Disk**: Block storage for VMs.

- **Queue**: Messaging store for asynchronous workflows.

Q: Can I access Azure Storage securely without exposing a key?
 A: Yes. Use **Shared Access Signatures (SAS)** or **Azure AD-based RBAC** for scoped and time-bound access.

Q: How do I scale an Azure SQL Database?
A: You can scale vertically by changing the pricing tier or DTUs/vCores, or horizontally using **Elastic Pools** and **Geo-Replication**.

AI and Serverless

Q: What is Azure Functions used for?
A: Azure Functions is a serverless compute platform that runs code in response to events. It's ideal for automation, data processing, and lightweight APIs.

Q: How do I integrate AI into my app using Azure?
A: Use **Cognitive Services** for pre-trained models or **Azure Machine Learning** to train and deploy custom models. Integrate via REST APIs or SDKs.

Q: Can I use GPT-4 with Azure?
A: Yes, through the **Azure OpenAI Service**, subject to approval. It enables you to access models like GPT-4 for chat, summarization, translation, and generation tasks.

Support and Troubleshooting

Q: How do I get support from Microsoft?
A: Use the **Help + support** blade in the Azure Portal to create a support request. Choose the appropriate severity and provide as much detail as possible.

Q: Is there a way to simulate changes before applying them?
A: Yes. Use the **What-If** feature in ARM/Bicep deployments to preview changes before execution:

```
az deployment group what-if --resource-group myRG --template-file main.bicep
```

Q: How do I report a platform outage or issue?
A:

1. Check https://status.azure.com for global incidents.

2. Use **Azure Service Health** for tenant-specific alerts.

3. Contact support for region-specific service degradation.

Summary

This FAQ section is designed to provide instant clarity on frequent Azure questions that arise during both learning and implementation. Azure is a vast platform, and even experienced users need quick answers from time to time. By bookmarking this section and referring to it regularly, you'll improve your fluency in Azure's terminology, tooling, and best practices. Whether troubleshooting, planning an architecture, or studying for certification, these questions and answers are practical companions in your cloud journey.

www.ingramcontent.com/pod-product-compliance
Lightning Source LLC
LaVergne TN
LVHW051432050326
832903LV00030BD/3043